D0061975

Powerfully
Simple Meetings
Your Guide to Fewer, Faster
More Focused Business Meetings

Peter Kidd & Bryan Field

Copyright © 2014 MeetingResult
Updated September 2015

All rights reserved.

ISBN: 0-9890945-0-2
ISBN-13: 978-0-9890945-0-4

DEDICATION

This book is dedicated to all the middle-management warriors in corporate America who regularly suffer through aimless, unproductive and wasteful business meetings. We aspire for the contents of this book to bring you hope for a better work day in the near future.

CONTENTS

ACKNOWLEDGMENTS

First and foremost we give thanks and praise to the Lord our God for blessing us with the ideas and experiences captured in this book, and the passion to share them. Thank you to our beautiful wives, Shiloh and Andrea, for loving and supporting us through our crazy entrepreneurial pursuits. Thank you to our children: Isabelle, Mason, Johnny, Reagan, Gigi, Endale, Eli, Esme and Hollyn. We are thankful for you and your sacrifices while your dads spent countless hours researching and writing the pages that follow. It is our honor and blessing to raise you. To our dear colleague, John Norton, for being the perfect addition to our MeetingResult team. Lastly we want to thank our colleagues, clients and coworkers who taught us the good, the bad and outright ugly aspects of meeting management, that we might design and offer the powerful solutions provided in this book.

Peter Kidd & Bryan Field

INTRODUCTION

If you don't have time to do it right,
when will you have time to do it over?

—John Wooden

If wasting time was a criminal offense, meetings would rank #1 on the FBI's Ten Most Wanted list.

Countless articles, blog posts and books have been written on various "tips and tricks" for conducting better business meetings. A simple Google search on *meeting tips and tricks* will return nearly 18 million hits. With so much information and so many "tricks," one would hope that these shortcuts have led to great strides in corporate meeting productivity. Yet the research reveals that the quality of our business meetings is no better today than it was twenty years ago, and is in fact getting worse.

While many great ideas are contained in some of these writings, they fail to provide comprehensive end-to-end method(s) that solve the fundamental challenges with meetings once and for all. That's why we wrote this book.

We all know that meetings are a basic fact of business life. They have been an essential business tool for centuries and remain a critical ingredient to corporate collaboration, innovation and overall execution. Despite technological advances in communication tools (for example, voicemail, email, instant messaging), meetings continue to consume a massive amount of time, as they remain an essential vehicle for collaborating on business challenges and opportunities. According to research presented in the May 2014 *Harvard Business Review* (*HBR*), titled "Your Scarcest Resource:"

> *On average, senior executives devote more than two days every week to meetings involving three or more coworkers, and 15% of an organization's collective time is spent in meetings—a percentage that has increased every year since 2008.*

Yet the overwhelming consensus among business professionals is that meetings are an inefficient drain on time and resources. The same *HBR* article noted

> *that senior executives rated more than half the meetings they attended as "ineffective" or "very ineffective."*

Whether you spend your meeting time in the boardroom, a conference room or a virtual meeting space, the productivity drain caused by ineffective meetings is widely acknowledged and reluctantly tolerated. Like excessive wait times at the Department of Motor Vehicles or endless delays at airport security, the depiction of the "meeting" has been relegated to a mere punch line, unfitting of such a necessary and costly business tool.

When was the last time you heard people comment that they *get to go* to a meeting? How often do you see disappointment in the faces of your colleagues when their meetings are cancelled? What other type of life experiences do you get *called to* besides meetings? The principal's office? To testify? Jury duty? Not exactly life's most eagerly anticipated activities. Chances are if you are reading this book, you already agree the business-meeting paradigm needs a major productivity makeover to achieve its full potential.

While it is clear that we have considerable problems with the effectiveness of our meetings, much of our frustration has been misdirected toward the meeting "vehicle" versus the "operation" of that vehicle. However indicting meetings for their ineffectiveness is like blaming an automobile for driving the wrong direction. Our course is not determined by the vehicle but in its operation, and therefore with its operator.

The purpose of this book is to provide you (the operator) with a simple yet powerful system that can immediately improve the end-to-end business meeting process in your organization. We call this system Powerfully Simple Meetings or PSM.

For most of our early careers, the cofounders of MeetingResult were stuck in conference rooms just like yours. We sat through unproductive, unplanned, unstandardized and over-attended meetings that drove ambiguous outcomes while consuming a lot of our "real work" time. We saw action items, decisions and ideas spark to life only to fade from a lack of meeting follow-up and accountability. And we naively accepted the status quo of meeting performance believing "that's just the way it is."

However, as we grew in our careers as leaders and project management professionals, we realized a desperate need to change the status quo of our own meetings. Like a saw to a carpenter, great business meetings are an essential tool that project managers use to deliver successful projects. We witnessed our share of failed projects and we knew if we didn't sharpen our tools and techniques, our projects would follow the common path of failure (that is, over budget, behind schedule, missed objectives).

We started by developing a meeting process that optimized our project performance. We were focused on bringing the highest level of clarity, accountability and effectiveness to our own meetings. We did extensive research, modeled the best meeting leaders and continued to improve our process through trial and error. We extensively studied what works (and what doesn't) and we applied these principles firsthand to deliver results in conference rooms and boardrooms just like yours. We received recognition and promotions largely in part to our ability to run great business meetings.

After decades of experience managing literally thousands of meetings, we decided it was time to share this knowledge that revolutionized our professional lives. We packaged our meeting process into a powerfully simple meeting (PSM) system that will enable you and your organization to conduct fewer, faster, more-focused meetings.

Whether in a project, sales or operations environment, it gives us great satisfaction to see leaders implement our meeting process and reap the benefits that virtually anyone can achieve if they consistently follow the principles and processes described in this book. It's our belief that there are two essential components that must come together for anyone to be a great meeting leader:

1. You need proven strategies for conducting great meetings and the skills to execute those strategies.

2. You need discipline in applying what you learn, consistency in sticking with the process and a continued drive for improvement.

So let's make a deal with each other. This book will take care of the number one component. We will impart everything we have learned through conducting thousands of business meetings during the past two decades. After reading this book you will be equipped with the principles, tools and techniques you need to be able to:

- Immediately conduct fewer, faster, and measurably more-productive business meetings in virtually any business context (for example, project meetings, sales meetings, staff meetings).

- Ensure clear meeting outcomes are efficiently captured and communicated with your stakeholders.

- Optimize your meeting attendance and significantly reduce the person hours that your organization invests in meetings.

- Improve your meeting facilitation skills by focusing on the four essential skills of any great meeting leader.

- Streamline the follow-up of meeting assignments and ensure that key actions and deliverables no longer "fall through the cracks."

- Differentiate yourself as a professional meeting leader.

- Evaluate your current meeting process and quickly implement this system without a cumbersome "culture change" initiative.

The number two component is your responsibility. While our meeting system is simple, it does require effort, especially in the early stages of your learning. Just as getting in shape isn't always easy, and is usually the most difficult during the first two weeks of exercise, achieving fitness in your meetings will require a little work upfront. Rest assured that the payoff will be worth it.

We applaud you for taking the first step and picking up this book. The next step is to take the fundamentals that you will learn in this book and apply them to every meeting that you have from this day forward.

Let's agree to hold each other accountable on this path toward *Powerfully Simple Meetings*. Please contact us and let us know about your successes and challenges. Knowing that we have improved the quality of your work life is the greatest reward we could ever receive for sharing the contents of this book.

To support you further, we've developed additional training videos, templates, and tools to help our PSM readers lead the most productive meeting imaginable. You can access these complimentary resources at http://meetingresult.com/psmmember.

Also, as a PSM book purchaser, you get an exclusive offer to try our Web-based meeting management software.

Just go to http://meetingresult.com/psmmember to learn more.

—Bryan Field & Peter Kidd
Cofounders, MeetingResult LLC

1 MEETING CONTEXT

When you do the common things in life in an uncommon way,
you will command the attention of the world.

—George Washington Carver

Before we dive too deeply into the details of meeting management, let's establish some needed context regarding the types of meetings that we're focused on in the pages of this book.

According to a recent Microsoft survey, there are an estimated 11 million meetings conducted each day in the United States. That is roughly 3 billion meetings per year in the United States alone. A staggering amount of time is pouring into meetings each day, but what exactly are we really referring to when we talk about "meetings."

If you stop to think about it for a moment, you will soon realize that there are so many different types of meetings with a variety of uses, formats and contexts. People "meet" for lunch, participate in homeowner association (HOA) meetings, board of directors meetings, executive committee meetings, sales meetings, project meetings, conferences, conference calls, webinars, staff meetings, one-on-one meetings, and the list goes on and on.

While all of these business activities can be grouped under a broad definition of "meetings," they also can have vastly different applications, and therefore different strategies for improving outcomes and performance. At MeetingResult we view meetings in three basic categories: social, informational, and collaborative meetings. Each of these meeting categories maintains their own unique characteristics, and each has their rightful place on the schedules of millions of professionals each day.

However it's important that you understand the difference. Our objective in categorizing these meetings is to help you distinguish among the types of meetings in which you participate, and specifically to assist you in applying the strategies, tools and processes needed to optimize performance in *collaborative* meetings.

Three Categories of Meetings

Social Meetings. These meetings are primarily relational in nature and center around a conversation or series of conversations. Social meetings involve two or more attendees and they tend to be more informal and are therefore less structured than the other meeting categories. While these meetings can certainly drive action and decision, their primary focus is typically more about developing business relationships and rapport than driving specific deliverables. Classic examples of meetings that fall into this category include lunch meetings, coffee appointments, networking events or even some one-on-one staff meetings.

Informational Meetings. As the name implies, informational meetings are mainly focused on sharing information from a central source (or sources) to other meeting attendees. Information is primarily shared uni-directionally in the form of a presentation or lecture, therefore attendee collaboration tends to be at a minimum. These meetings are less relational than social meetings because of the focus on information sharing versus relationship building. Classic examples of these types of meetings include town hall meetings, project briefings, instructional webinars or group presentations.

Collaborative Meetings. These meetings tend to be interactive and action-oriented group gatherings. Their purpose is to align stakeholders while provoking ideas, decision and action. Specifically we define a collaborative meeting as:

> *A collaborative gathering of two or more people designed to advance an organization, project or opportunity by driving discussion, decision and action, while fostering team alignment and accountability.*

Simply put, a collaborative meeting is about aligning a group of people around a body of work in order to drive business forward. While there might be social or information aspects to the meeting, the primary purpose is to push work forward. Classic examples of these meetings include project team meetings, client sales meetings, executive team meetings, staff meetings, strategy meetings, brainstorming meetings and board of directors meetings.

Virtually any individual meeting can fall into each of the aforementioned categories depending on the content and objectives. For example, there are instances where a "sales meeting" could be social, informational or collaborative depending on what's going on in the meeting. The same is true for executive team, board of directors or project team meetings. Our goal is to be cognizant of the type of meeting you are managing so that you can leverage the most appropriate strategies and tools.

PSM Focus on Collaborative Meetings

As we continue our journey toward *Powerfully Simple Meetings,* it's important to note that the strategies, skills and tools you will acquire in this book are most applicable to collaborative meetings. While the resources contained herein can still be used for social and informational meetings, they are specifically designed for the complexity and dynamics associated with the management of collaborative meetings.

For the remainder of this book when we use the word "meeting" we are specifically referring to a collaborative meeting.

As mentioned earlier, a key component of a collaborative meeting is the focus on advancing business forward. This implies the meeting will involve decisions being made, actions being tasked, important ideas being generated, problems raised, questions asked and answered, and information shared throughout the course of the meeting. While every collaborative meeting does not always contain all of these attributes (for example, not every meeting will lead to a decision), we would expect the majority to be present in virtually any legitimate collaborative meeting.

Collaborative meetings drive business and are the most complex of the three meeting categories previously mentioned. They require strategy, process, skill and tools to execute effectively. These are the meetings where *Powerfully Simple Meetings* can have the most profound impact on the performance of you and your teams.

As a reminder, we've developed exclusive training videos, tools, and other resources for our PSM readers at our website. You can access these complimentary resources at http://meetingresult.com/psmmember.

Peter Kidd & Bryan Field

2 MEETING PROBLEMS

I just hate meetings.

—J. K. Rowling

How can something as fundamental as meetings be so universally despised?

The answer is simple. The vast majority of business professionals believe meetings are a waste of their precious time and energy. Most of us are familiar with the common meeting complaints:

- *Too many meetings cut into my "real work."*

- *Meetings are way too long.*

- *Meetings are a waste of my time; there's a lot of talk but nothing really gets done.*

- *Meetings are poorly planned. Sometimes I wonder why we're even meeting.*

- *People miss meetings or show up late and we waste time bringing them up to speed.*

- *There are way too many people in our meetings.*

- *We spend so much time rehashing topics from prior meetings and never make decisions.*

- *People always hijack the meeting for their personal agendas and derail everyone else.*

- *There's no follow-up after the meeting; everyone goes off and does their own thing.*

Do any of these sound familiar to you? What else would you add? This list is by no means complete but it is representative of the poor execution that's obstructing the meeting process.

Evaluating collective meeting criticism reveals that an ineffective meeting culture creates massive waste of corporate resources and drains employee engagement.

Several prominent meeting surveys report meetings as a top time waster among workers surveyed. Microsoft surveyed more than 38,000 people in 200 countries. The survey respondents reported that they felt 69 percent of the time they spent in meetings was unproductive. In a 2012 study by career site Salary.com "Too many meetings" was identified by 47 percent of workers as the number-one time waster at the office.

Throughout the years, meeting management ineptitude takes a toll. Meetings that lack clear vision and direction and fail to engage attendees ultimately have a negative impact on company performance and employee job satisfaction.

Good News, Bad News

Let's start with the bad news. Organizations have been trying to solve meeting-related problems for decades, and so far little progress has been made. Countless pet projects have been mobilized to improve meeting effectiveness, yet few organizations have been able to produce a legitimately productive meeting culture. While there are pockets of high performance, overall it is extremely rare to find an organization that has cracked the code for consistent meeting effectiveness.

A few years ago, we worked with a large financial services organization that readily admitted to having a materially deficient meeting culture. The inefficiency and waste extended all the way from the mailroom to the boardroom. Too many meetings, taking too much time, with too many people, producing too few results.

The organization's approach to solving its meeting problems was to simply treat the symptoms of the problems by mandating them away. The chief executive officer (CEO) of this Fortune 100 company issued a decree that all one-hour meetings should be reduced to forty-five minutes, to improve productivity and allow travel between meetings. He added that all meetings must have an agenda, and that attendees must show up on time.

Incredibly, with all of the resources available to this organization, *this* was the corporate meeting strategy—show up on time for shorter meetings with an agenda.

How do you think this worked? Right, it didn't.

Other organizations take a less autocratic approach and encourage the need for good *facilitation* practices to treat the symptoms of their meeting problems. They focus on the importance of leveraging soft skills for effective meeting management (for example, involve all participants in the discussion, keep the discussion on target, strive for conclusion, keep the discussion positive) while stressing the need to manage the meeting attendees with facilitated exercises and personality management.

To be clear, we respect and value the need for good meeting facilitation. In fact, we believe it is an important component of effective meeting management. However we must acknowledge that the historical practice of addressing meeting productivity problems with meeting facilitation techniques simply doesn't go far enough to improve the meeting process. Meetings need more than good facilitation to surmount the obstacles that have bogged down meeting effectiveness for decades.

The good news is that these meeting problems are solvable. Each of the meeting complaints mentioned earlier in this chapter can be addressed, and meetings can be the productive organizational tool they are intended to be. But to solve our meeting problems we must look beyond the symptoms of ineffectiveness. Taking cough medicine might provide a short-term fix, but to the person with a bronchial infection it will do nothing to solve the underlying problem. If we are going to cure our meeting problems, we must treat the underlying infection.

The goal of any meeting management strategy must be first to identify and then defuse the fundamental problems at the core of each meeting. This begins with an important distinction. Symptoms of poor meetings are often outside of the control of the meeting manager. However, the root cause problems are well within the control of the meeting leader to manage. This means the meeting leader holds the keys for unlocking meeting productivity and is not at the mercy of the organizational meeting culture or attendee personalities. If a meeting leader is given authority to manage a meeting, then he or she is absolutely capable of impelling its effectiveness.

We'll cover the root cause problems in a moment, but first take a few minutes to think of a successful business meeting where results were generated, progress was made, people contributed in meaningful ways and you had a sense of pride and accomplishment. Put this book aside for just a moment, and recall how the meeting was conducted and how you reacted.

If you cannot remember a successful meeting, imagine what one would look like. Picture a meeting that would be the prototype for organization, collaboration, productivity and performance. As you recall or imagine this successful meeting, consider the following questions:

1. How closely aligned were the attendees on the objectives for the meeting? Did most everyone know what the group was looking to accomplish or did everyone have their own agendas?

2. How much ownership and accountability was taking place in the meeting? Were people highly accountable or were they dodging their responsibilities?

3. What about attendance? Were the right people in the room or were ancillary attendees involved?

4. How clear were the results of the meeting? Was there clarity about decisions made and the tasks assigned? Or did the meeting close with participants left to their own understandings?

5. Did you need to schedule a follow-up meeting to rehash the same content or were you able to make forward progress?

If you are like most of our clients, you already possess a vision of what a successful meeting looks like and how it should function. However, like most of our clients, translating that vision into reality can be problematic if you don't understand the five root cause problems that are waiting to destroy your perfect meeting vision. We call these problems the five meeting killers.

The Meeting Killers

The following five "meeting killers" represent the root cause problems that must be neutralized for any organization to sustain a productive meeting management culture:

1. High Ambiguity

2. Limited Accountability

3. Over and Under Participation

4. Inadequate Process and Training

5. Insufficient Data

High Ambiguity

am·bi·gu·i·ty, noun

—doubtfulness or uncertainty of meaning or
intention: to speak with ambiguity;
an ambiguity of manner.
—dictionary.com

Ambiguity is the single most dangerous killer of
meeting effectiveness. It is the fog that exists in your
meeting space that creates uncertainty, uncertainty
leads to confusion, and confusion leads to inefficiency
and waste. Ambiguity can impact every single aspect
of your meeting performance, including:

- Objectives—why are we even having this
  meeting?

- Outcomes—what was decided and what are
  next steps?

- Accountability—who is responsible?

- Timing—when are tasks due?

- Meaning—what does that statement or that
  acronym mean?

Have you ever left a meeting and had a follow-up
conversation with another attendee who had a
completely different impression about the outcomes

of the meeting? Several years ago we witnessed a senior executive officer at a multibillion-dollar corporation make a critical decision about the direction of an important corporate project. Several members of team around the conference table accepted the decision and left the room with expectations to deliver on the change immediately. Shortly after the meeting the senior executive learned of the team beginning to take action against the decision and immediately put a stop to it. When questioned why he changed his mind, his response was "I never made a final decision, I was just thinking through my options." Ambiguity is a meeting killer.

At times we see meeting ambiguity as a fairly unintentional but costly factor as noted in the example above. Other times ambiguity is used intentionally by meeting attendees to avoid the accountability that comes with precision and clarity. Unfortunately in low-accountability business cultures, ambiguity provides a safe hiding place from responsibility. When there is uncertainty in a meeting about who is on point for delivering work, when specific actions are due and overall performance expectations, it makes it much easier for individuals to do as they please, and more difficult for them to "fail."

Considered this way, ambiguity is a friend of the elusive attendee, and an enemy to those driving for results.

Limited Accountability

ac·count·a·ble, adjective

> —subject to the obligation to report, explain, or justify something; responsible; answerable
> —dictionary.com

A common killer of meetings performance involves a fundamental lack of personal accountability throughout the meeting process, both on the part of meeting leaders and attendees. Participants who consistently show up late, unprepared and distracted contribute to this problem just as much as the meeting leader who arrives without a thoughtful plan and approach for maximizing the use of stakeholders' precious time.

The importance of creating a culture of accountability cannot be understated. As identified in our definition of a collaborative meeting provided in chapter one, a meeting must "*[foster] team alignment and accountability.*" Fostering accountability means holding attendees responsible to adhere to decisions, take action and share the information necessary to move business forward.

On the one hand, a system of accountability confronts individuals that leverage ambiguity to avoid being held accountable. On the other hand, it addresses individuals of low accountability that make commitments (that is, accept action items, acknowledge deliverable dates and agree to decisions) but fail to follow through. Regardless of the situation, the goal is to ensure accountability is clear and develop a process to reinforce it.

There is an important distinction between enforcing accountability and having direct authority over an individual. A common misconception among meeting leaders is, "I can't hold attendees accountable because they don't report to me." But a skilled meeting leader uses the meeting process to bring stakeholders to account in a professional manner. You'll learn those skills throughout the pages of this book.

Over and Under Participation

par·tic·i·pate, verb

—to take or have a part or share,
as with others; partake; share
—dictionary.com

Have you ever been in a meeting and looked around the room and wondered why in the world are all these people in this meeting? Have you ever taken it a step further and estimated the cost of the meeting based on the time multiplied by an average salary for each person in the room. If you're reading this book, then our guess is that you've asked yourself one or both of these questions at some point in time.

Too many meeting participants bog down the meeting process and negatively impact morale and productivity. Part of the problem with over attendance is that the "over attendees" often feel the need to say something to justify their presence, which simply chews up precious time and hinders the productivity of the meeting.

In the most positive light, over attendance occurs when people have a legitimate need to hear the information that is being discussed in the meeting. Perhaps they don't need to contribute to the meeting objectives and agenda, but they do need to know the outcomes. In fairness to these people, they might be just trying to get the information they need to perform their jobs, as inefficient and disruptive as that might be.

Other examples of over attendance come from micromanaging bosses who want to be "in the know," freeloading attendees who simply want to look busy and appear important and others who just seem to indiscriminately show up at any meeting that someone invites them to attend. Don't we all have references for situations such as these?

On the flip side, under participation can also kill your meeting effectiveness if essential attendees do not show up for your key meetings. The obvious problem here is that you end up losing the knowledge, experience or decision-making authority that you expected this attendee to exhibit during the meeting. A second problem is the risk that these absent stakeholders shun ownership of the decisions and other content generated during the meeting—a problem akin to the accountability discussion above.

During a recent sales meeting with a government contractor, we got an earful from the contractor's team when we started speaking about the PSM approach to counteracting participation problems. They were lamenting the fact that their clients rarely showed up to key project meetings. Apparently the clients prefer to send consultants to attend in their place. These same clients would then throw up roadblocks when it came time to make important project decisions. They objected because "they were never included in the process." The result was significant project delays and cost overruns—all because stakeholder participation wasn't effectively managed throughout the project. For the record, this problem is not limited to the public sector, as most of us in the private sector know all too well.

By leveraging the PSM system, you'll learn strategies for optimizing meeting attendance and mitigating the corresponding risks.

Inadequate Process & Training

proc·ess, verb, adjective, noun

—a systematic series of actions directed to some end
—dictionary.com

Cultural norms for conducting meetings vary among industries and organizations, but a solid meeting process is vital for excellent meeting performance. Unfortunately few organizations have such a process. Imagine a major highway with no lines on the road and no posted signs on the shoulder. Now imagine a daily commute on this road with tens of thousands of other drivers who were never taught how to drive. How effectively would the traffic flow? How is this any different from the meeting process in most organizations? Inadequate process from under-equipped leaders is a meeting killer.

In our experience, the meeting process is generally left to the discretion of the individual meeting leader, rather than following a proven organizational process. Yet most business professionals have never received formal training about how to plan and run effective meetings. In a recent survey of our MeetingResult iPad application users, fewer than ten percent of users ever received training about conducting business meetings. Imagine the enormous amount of time invested in meetings each day, yet fewer than 10 percent of professionals ever receive training about how to conduct effective business meetings.

In some instances, a business meeting is treated like nothing more than a social group gathering. Stakeholders congregate at an arranged time and location to pontificate or bloviate on some business topic. If the stars align perfectly, perhaps progress will be made. This is a bit of a Wild West format, where outcomes are essentially left to chance.

A step up brings us to meetings that follow a basic agenda. These meetings use an agenda to guide the discussions and expectations of the meeting content. Agenda-driven meetings rely on the structure of key topics, input from topic leaders and teams, and allocated time to move the meeting forward.

Meetings that add additional structure with established objectives and meeting notes (or minutes) represent today's "gold standard" for meeting management. Unfortunately the perception of success for these meetings is often assessed on the level of effort and planning involved versus tangible results.

In each case, the meeting approach is falling short of the mark because of the absence of a fundamental process designed to drive results, minimize ambiguity, increase accountability, optimize attendance and capture essential data.

Insufficient Data

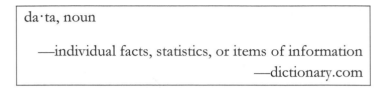

da·ta, noun

—individual facts, statistics, or items of information
—dictionary.com

Consider these questions:

- How many meetings do you conduct each year?

- How about your organization?

- How many person hours are consumed in these meetings?

- What content is generated in these meetings?

- What levels in the organization are attending the meetings?

- How often do they attend? How often do they fail to attend?

- What percentage of your meetings are collaborative versus informational?

Virtually no organization can answer all of these questions accurately. Minimal insight into the actual activities of our meetings is a key reason there has been such little improvement in the meeting process. For most organizations, the typical gauge for meeting success is how people *feel* about the meeting when it ends. Curiously, we rely on anecdotal emotional reaction to evaluate our meeting productivity.

Without a quantitative way to assess meeting performance, it's no wonder that we've languished in improving the process. In the words of the great management consultant Peter Drucker "If you can't measure it, you can't manage it." There's a really good reason that most people keep a scale in the bathroom. Whether or not we like the results, we are motivated to improve when we have a measurement of our performance (that is, data). Data, then, is a key ingredient in the recipe for ongoing meeting improvement. Yet its absence in today's meetings is a meeting killer.

Where Do We Go From Here?

Collectively, the five meeting killers represent the root cause problems that damage your meeting productivity and performance.

If you want to learn more about the specific killers that are impacting your meetings, we've developed an on-line assessment tool for PSM readers. This complimentary assessment will help you narrow-in on your specific challenges, and develop plans to improve your meeting effectiveness. Visit us at http://meetingresult.com/psmmember and we'll share more information about how to obtain this additional insight.

In the following chapters we will present the five core areas of meeting management practices that will help you to disarm the five meeting killers and enable you to deliver the most powerfully simple meetings imaginable. These components include:

1. Guiding Principles—these five guiding principles represent the foundational pillars on which all of PSM is based.

2. Meeting Process—the fundamental steps and strategies that you need to follow to execute consistently outstanding business meetings.

3. Leader Skills and Traits—the core competencies and skills you must continually sharpen to be the best meeting leader possible.

4. Plan for Getting Started—the strategy and steps for beginning the process of implementing PSM in your organization.

5. Available Technology—an overview of the tools available to fast-track your PSM journey and automate the meeting process.

3 GUIDING PRINCIPLES

Everything must be made as simple as possible.
But not simpler.

—Albert Einstein

The path to neutralizing meeting killers begins with embracing five guiding principles for running Powerfully Simple Meetings. These principles are the foundation upon which the remainder of the PSM system is based.

Figure 3.1. PSM Guiding Principles

#1 Champion Simplicity

It's should come as no surprise that a meeting management system called "Powerfully Simple Meetings" begins with a guiding principle of *champion simplicity*. This principle represents the foundation on which each of the other guiding principles stands. Champion simplicity means that our approach to managing meetings must (a) breakthrough the current paradigm and produce high performing meetings, and (b) must do so with relative ease of the meeting leader and attendees. In other words, the system must produce fewer, faster, more focused meetings without adding unnecessary complexity in the process.

We recently watched in amazement as one of our three-year-old sons grasped an iPhone and effortlessly navigated to his choice app (Disney Jr.) to watch his favorite show. Every now and again he would take a break from the show and intuitively navigate to the music library to play one of his favorite iTunes songs. What's more, he knew exactly how to turn the volume down when we asked him to keep quiet, and then crank it right back up when we weren't paying attention.

Though this little guy is oblivious to Apple's technology running the iPhone, he is able to work the phone with outstanding results. The brilliance of the iPhone is the way Apple combined the power and complexity of its brilliant technology with a simple, intuitive interface even a three year old can master.

In designing PSM we too strived to keep the complexity behind the scenes (that is, baked into the process itself) without jeopardizing performance. The result is a meeting management system that is relatively easy to learn and implement, but powerful enough to have a profound impact on the quality of your meeting productivity. As you begin leveraging PSM, it's important to avoid the tendency to add more complexity to the process.

#2 Focus on Results

An essential element of any great meeting is a continual focus on achieving results. While this might seem like common sense, it is surprisingly not so common. A results focus begins with identifying and maintaining a clear understanding of meeting objectives and the anticipated outcomes. Aligning meeting attendees on the desired outcomes, keeping them focused on these outcomes and documenting these outcomes is "a continual focus on results."

While it is standard to start a meeting with a sense of purpose or even an agenda, maintaining that focus throughout the meeting takes a concentrated effort. Once initiated, meetings often behave more like a tree branch floating down a river than a team of whitewater rafters paddling toward their destination.

The tree branch tends to get caught on the riverbank or break to pieces in the falls.

A focus on results means actively managing meetings with a list of clear objectives to achieve a set of decisive results—ever paddling toward your destination.

#3 Optimize Attendance

Holding a meeting without the right attendees can be like attempting open-heart surgery without an anesthesiologist in the operating room, then inviting family members in to lean over the surgeon's shoulder to watch. There are a specific set of people who are required to be in that operating room in order to ensure a successful outcome, and there is little room for extraneous staff. To keep our meetings focused on achieving our objectives, we must treat our meeting rooms more like operating rooms and less like hospital waiting rooms where most anyone is welcome.

While we might not be performing heart surgery, the same principles apply when it comes to ensuring we have the right people in the room. Our outcomes and productivity rest on our ability to invite only those people required to successfully accomplish our objective(s).

Optimizing attendance means inviting the people to the meeting required to *contribute to the achievement* of your meeting objectives. Others stakeholders should be kept informed about the output of the meeting. This approach is an essential component of the PSM value proposition designed to save meeting hours.

Optimizing attendance requires a meeting leader to distinguish between those who "contribute" and those who "consume." Contributors are individuals who are required to provide input that is essential to achieving the objective(s) of the meeting. They could be a decision maker, a subject matter expert or a member of the team who is directly involved with the subject of the meeting. The bottom line is that they have input that is required. Consumers are individuals who might have a need to know the outcome of the meeting but they aren't needed to contribute to the stated objective(s) of the meeting.

We will discuss meeting attendance further in chapter four.

#4 Drive Clarity

We recently participated in a half-day meeting with the senior executive team of a multibillion-dollar organization. During the meeting one of the executives presented a proposal for a project that had the potential to earn the organization $50M each year. The executive laid out her expected outcome for the presentation, which included a go or no-go decision to proceed with the project, approval for the human resources required to implement the project and recommendations for an alternative approach if needed.

We watched as an eight-member senior executive team invested forty-five minutes listening to the presentation and providing valuable feedback. Afterward, we asked the presenting executive what marching orders she took away from the meeting. She explained she wasn't "certain" about the direction she was given. She believed that overall the team agreed with the approach, but she was not sure if they had actually made a decision. Her plan was to go back to the team during the next meeting (next month) and clarify.

The obvious problem in this case was the failure to obtain the required clarity regarding a go versus no-go decision before the meeting adjourned. During the follow-up meeting she learned that she had already obtained approval to proceed with the project.

To achieve consistently great meetings we must consistently *drive for clarity*. Look at the inefficiency and lost opportunity exemplified in the example above. Think about the investment of time to conduct a follow-up meeting and the opportunity cost of delaying the project by a month.

Our meeting rooms are filled with jargon, shorthand and acronyms that can confuse communication and inhibit productivity. Attention to clarity combats the tendency for vague language, unclear direction and uncertain accountability. Driving for clarity better enables meeting managers to support stakeholder discussion by driving the team to cleaner, clearer, more precise communication.

#5 Capture Meeting Assets

The principle of meeting assets is based on the belief that the purpose of any business meeting is to generate value for the organization. By definition an asset is an item of value owned by an entity. In PSM, we capture this value in the form of "meeting assets" that represent the intellectual property that surfaces during the course of a meeting. Simply put, meeting assets are the fruit of the meeting and must be appropriately harvested by the meeting leader.

Chapter five includes a full discussion about the mechanics of using meeting assets, but for now we need to be clear that business meetings are more than intangible discussion, status updates and debate. They are vehicles that generate intellectual property in the form of thought, action and decision. This intellectual property must be captured, owned and communicated in order for it to retain value.

Consider a project team that makes an important decision during the course of a business meeting. That decision represents an important business asset (that is, item of worth) that can now be utilized by the organization to address a business problem. The organization invested capital resources (that is, salary, materials, overhead) to identify the asset so that it can be put into service. The problem we have today is that organizations fail to treat business meetings as asset-generating vehicles. As a result, the intellectual property is frequently mismanaged or just plain missed.

If your business meetings are not generating tangible assets for your organization, then you must consider why you are meeting in the first place. Are your meetings truly collaborative or are they strictly social or informational? If your meetings are intended to be collaborative and yet you're not generating assets, then you're reading the right book!

The type of meeting assets that are generated in business meetings vary across organizations and meetings. For instance, sales team meetings are likely to generate some different assets than project team meetings. Regardless of your organization, business function or meeting type, if you are conducting truly collaborative meetings then you are most certainly surfacing valuable meeting assets. The question is whether or not you're effectively capturing these assets and realizing their full value. We'll explore meeting assets in more detail throughout chapter five.

With the foundation of these guiding principles set, it's time to discuss the PSM meeting process that leverages these principles.

As a reminder, we've developed exclusive training videos, tools, and other resources for our PSM readers at our website. You can access these complimentary resources at http://meetingresult.com/psmmember.

.

4 MEETING PROCESS

If I had eight hours to chop down a tree,
I'd spend six hours sharpening my ax.

—Abraham Lincoln

Great meetings rarely just happen by chance. They
are designed and managed by following a specific
protocol that produces consistently great results. With
PSM, we have distilled the essentials of the meeting
process into a streamlined system that empowers our
clients to take control of their meeting performance.
Each step in the process can take anywhere from a
few minutes to a few days depending on the
circumstances of the meeting, and the bottom line is
that each step must be completed in order to
consistently manage outstanding business meetings.

Planning

Plans are of little importance, but planning is essential.

—Winston Churchill

Great business meetings start with thoughtful
planning. We are always dumbfounded when we see
business executives "winging" important meetings.

Either too busy, too confident or too careless to properly plan, they leave their colleagues' time and productivity to chance. Can you imagine a professional football quarterback beginning a drive without a thoughtful plan? We all know that he would have little chance for success. The old axiom holds true in football as well as in business meetings; "if you're failing to plan, then you're planning to fail." Yet for some strange reason many organizations tolerate this lackluster behavior.

On the other hand, there are conscientious managers who are adamant about the need to have an agenda for their meetings. These managers at least invest the time to think through the meeting topics, sequence and the allotted time to cover them. While this agenda-only approach is more effective than "winging it," there are big holes that need to be filled in to ensure optimal performance that drives the results we desire. To that end, PSM divides planning into three components: meeting approach, stakeholders, and logistics.

Meeting Approach

Meeting approach begins with thinking through and documenting the meeting objectives. A common problem we see in meeting planning is the tendency to start planning with the creation of an agenda without first considering the objectives. That's like getting in your car and beginning to drive without first determining where you really want to go.

Setting objectives is accomplished by considering two basic questions: What specifically am I seeking to accomplish during my meeting? What do I want others to focus on during the meeting? Meeting objectives are comprised of statements that complete the following sentence: The objective of this meeting is to_____. Examples of these objectives include:

- Obtain final approval to proceed with the next design phase of the ABC project.

- Determine client needs for information technology (IT) services and establish criteria for us to demonstrate our capability to meet those needs.

- Communicate the current state of the XYZ implementation and obtain insight from attendees on resolving our two resource issues.

- Decide on a specific course of action for remediating our two key audit findings.

The importance of establishing meeting objectives cannot be understated. In order to be certain that everyone in the meeting is pointed toward the same target, you must define the target. The interesting thing about documenting meeting objectives is that the more difficult they are for you to define, the more important it is that you lay them out clearly. Keep in mind that one of our guiding principles is to bring clarity to an intrinsically ambiguous process. If the meeting manager is not clear on the objectives, then how can you expect anyone else to stay on target? Setting and communicating clear objectives is a critical first step toward that end.

Once you are crystal clear on the objectives for your meeting you are in a position to map out the best course for accomplishing those objectives (that is, your agenda). Your agenda represents the components and sequence of the meeting needed to achieve your stated objectives.

Each meeting must have a minimum of one agenda item that supports one or more meeting objectives. If an agenda item doesn't support an objective, then you have either an unnecessary agenda item or inadequate meeting objectives.

Each agenda item should consist of:

- Agenda Item Overview—a short description that makes it crystal clear what will be covered during this part of the meeting.

- Leaders—individual(s) responsible for leading the topic and guiding its results.

- Time—an estimated amount of time allocated to cover the agenda item.

The order of your agenda is an important component of the planning process. There are many factors that contribute to deciding the optimal order of an agenda (for example, priority of the topic relative to meeting objectives, decisions required as input to other agenda items, attendee meeting schedules). There are few absolute rules when it comes to deciding the order of an agenda. The only absolute is that the meeting manager applies the necessary forethought to manage an efficient, productive meeting.

A key point is that the meeting agenda should be prepared and distributed to meeting attendees prior to the beginning of the meeting. Although lead time on distribution of meeting agendas will vary among meetings and companies, twenty-four hours is a good rule of thumb.

Visit <u>http://meetingresult.com/psmmember</u> to download a complimentary meeting agenda template for your use.

The final component in developing the meeting approach relates to meeting materials. The key questions to be addressed include:

- What materials are required to support my meeting objectives and agenda?

- When do I need to distribute these materials to attendees?

Determining what materials are required to support your agenda and how they will be utilized is ultimately determined by the meeting manager and the agenda topic leaders.

We believe that familiarizing attendees with the meeting content as early as possible is generally in the best interest of driving results. However we recognize this is a decision best left to the realities of the organization and discretion of the meeting manager. Therefore we will refrain from over-prescribing a standard approach to content distribution.

Meeting Stakeholders

Once your meeting content is planned, you are in a position to determine who to involve in your meeting. Failure to appropriately complete this step can result in a significant waste of time and resources. As mentioned in the previous chapter on guiding principles, the PSM system distinguishes between two types of stakeholders when organizing and executing your meetings:

Attendees. These are individuals whose contribution is essential for obtaining your meeting objectives.

Subscribers. These are individuals who have a vested interest in the content and results of the meeting, but whose attendance is not required to meet the objectives. Essentially subscribers function as consumers of meeting information and our focus is on keeping them informed. We see many instances in client organizations where nearly half of the individuals attending the meeting are really subscribers who don't actually need to be present. Subscriber time can be much better utilized by providing these individuals the information they need after the meeting.

As we progress through this book, you will soon see how the PSM system ensures that subscribers receive all the relevant information they need through a clear, concise approach.

In many organizations we see the meeting invitation net cast so wide as to become overly inclusive. While inclusiveness in the right context is a great principle, when it comes to meetings it proves to be a colossal waste of time. For those people not contributing to meeting objectives, it amounts to time better spent elsewhere. For those who are contributing, it often bogs down the meeting process

On occasion, there are exceptions to the proper parameters of determining who should be invited to attend your meetings. It can be a matter of providing individuals with face-time, exposure or professional development by allowing them to listen to the discussion. Other times the decision to invite an otherwise unnecessary attendee is a matter of internal politics. While these isolated instances exist, the meeting manager should strive for a clean delineation between attendees and subscribers wherever possible.

There is one final category of meeting stakeholders that bears mentioning—a category we call "taggers." Taggers are third-party individuals whose attendance is not required to meet the objectives of the meeting (that is, they are not attendees) and are not known to be consumers of the meeting information (that is, they are not known subscribers). However, during the course of a meeting, taggers are identified as potential stakeholders who might need to be informed of certain meeting content. An example of a tagger would be:

> Attendee: *We can't move forward until the compliance report is reviewed by Legal.*
>
> Meeting Leader: *Who's on point for getting that report to Legal for review?*
>
> Attendee: *Oh, Janet Miller in Finance is supposed to be preparing and submitting that report*
>
> Meeting Leader: *Does Janet know she's on point?*
>
> Attendee: *I think so?*
>
> Meeting Leader: *I'll make certain she knows.*

We will discuss how to manage taggers in chapter five. For now we need to at least be aware of this category of stakeholder who might need to know about a specific piece of information that surfaced in your meeting. These people might not need all of the output from the meeting, but they should at least be informed that there is an expectation that they are aware of, or they need to do something.

In the example above, the meeting leader simply needs to notify Janet Miller about the expectations that she is going to send the compliance report to Legal. If Janet is aware of this expectation, great. If she's not aware, then it's a good thing she was notified.

Meeting Logistics

The final step in the planning process is completing the meeting logistics. Logistics work covers the basics of finalizing the meeting date, time, location and duration based on the previous planning work mentioned above. It might include secondary steps to outline expectations for attendance, delegates (that is, delegates are welcomed or they aren't), pre-work or pre-read expectations, material distribution, catering, equipment, post-meeting documentation and reporting.

PSM does not prescribe any hard rules about managing meeting logistics, other than that they need to be done, and done well! Even a well-planned meeting can be overshadowed if a conference room is too small, too hot, or doesn't contain the equipment (for example, a projector) needed to execute the meeting. Meeting leaders are responsible for ensuring every detail of the meeting is considered and covered.

Execution

Out of intense complexities, intense simplicities emerge.

—Winston Churchill

The meeting execution phase takes place from the time a meeting begins until the time a meeting is adjourned. Simply put, the execution phase is about implementing the planned meeting approach, leading and aligning stakeholders and capturing the value generated along the way. Effective execution relies on a focused leader who drives results throughout the entire meeting process.

We recently participated in a two-hour meeting with ten attendees assembled to address an emerging regulatory challenge. In this case the meeting leader did a good job planning this important meeting. He thoughtfully established the objectives for the meeting and creating an agenda to support those objectives. He also effectively managed all the meeting logistics and had the right attendees present and equipped to execute a productive meeting.

However problems began to emerge quickly as the team initiated its first agenda item. What soon became obvious was that the meeting leader believed his job was essentially done once he completed the planning process and got everyone in the room. It was as if he viewed his role more as a valet attendant than an actual chauffeur. He was too eager to give up the keys and allow the stakeholders to take the driver's seat.

Throughout the course of this meeting, the meeting leader retracted into a bystander role versus an actual leader. What he did not recognize was that he was responsible to *drive results throughout the entire meeting process.* This is a vital responsibility that does not end after a meeting is planned and continues after the meeting has been completed and attendees have left the room.

In fairness to this meeting leader, he simply did not know his responsibilities. It's not as if he had ever been trained, or his boss clearly instructed him on the expectations of his meeting role. Unfortunately though, his lack of understanding led to several common mistakes that waste valuable time. A couple of key mistakes we witnessed include:

- Failure to redirect the discussion as the dialogue drifted off course to sidebar conversations and to bring everyone back to the agenda and objectives.

- Failure to ensure attendee alignment by actively clarifying discussion that was unclear or unsettled (particularly as it related to decisions and action commitments).

- Failure to effectively manage the agenda by alerting presenters who were going way over time (without a compelling need to do so). As a result there was not enough time to address other important agenda items.

- Failure to manage the important information that surfaced throughout the meeting. As important ideas were raised, decisions made and assignments surfaced, he neglected to capture this activity. In essence he left all these important points to reside in the short-term memories and notepads of the meeting attendees.

- Failure to clarify the key outcomes from the meeting and align the next steps going forward.

Not surprisingly this same team found itself in another meeting two weeks later rehashing much of the same information. The attendees wasted valuable time as they tried to recall what they discussed and decided on two weeks earlier. Each attendee maintained a slightly different recollection of "where we ended up."

Does this scenario sound at all familiar? Unfortunately for most organizations this is a daily experience. However, utilizing PSM you can put an end to this madness.

The meeting execution phase is where the PSM system diverges significantly from the status quo of meeting management. From the time a meeting begins until the time it is adjourned, and everything in between—our focus is on driving our attendees through a process to efficiently attain our meeting objectives while capturing the essential value generated along the way. The execution phase of PSM has three components: initiation, body, and conclusion. Collectively these practices represent the structure for executing great meetings.

Meeting Initiation

Meeting initiation is about providing the context for the meeting so that everyone is aligned and ready to drive toward the meeting objectives. In a standard one-hour meeting, at least the first three to five minutes should be allocated to defining the context of the meeting.

> *Example: As you might know we had a security breech in our website over the weekend. So the focus of our time here today will be to brief you on the details of the breech and obtain your input on a plan to remedy the situation going forward. To that end, our agenda is to . . .*

Even if the agenda and objectives are properly distributed prior to the meeting, you should avoid the assumption that everyone in the room has the same understanding of purpose and approach. The aim here is straightforward: to align attendees on the goals and task at hand.

Meeting initiation is the time for you to set expectations about the protocols, guidelines or special requests of your meeting (for example, hold your questions until the end, avoid checking email if possible, please help us stay on time). It's also a great time to ask if attendees have any other expectations, objectives or special circumstances (for example, need to step out of the meeting or leave early). Examples of meeting initiation questions/comments include:

- Is there anything else that you think we need to cover during our time today?

- Do you have any questions about our objectives?

- Is everyone onboard with what we're looking to accomplish?

- Does anyone need to leave early?

- Our agenda is tight today so please allow me to keep everyone on task with our agenda and objectives.

- Please refrain from checking your email or text messages because we really need your total focus to accomplish our objectives and avoid scheduling another meeting.

The final component of initiation is to take attendance. This step is as simple as it gets, but it needs to be done and it's good that attendees know you're doing it. Remember we're working to develop an environment of accountability in our meeting space and knowing who's attending and who isn't is an important component of this work. Tracking attendance is a small but important link in the chain of accountability.

Meeting Body

The body is the bulk of the meeting time and it is where the majority of the meeting value is created. As mentioned earlier, meeting leaders are responsible for leading the attendees through the agenda, toward the attainment of the meeting objectives and capturing all of the valuable insight that surfaces along the way. The body of the meeting involves two main functions for the meeting manager to lead: flow and capture.

Flow

The meeting manager is responsible to ensure that the meeting flows from initiation and drives toward the meeting objectives. Along the way attendees might veer off course. Flow consists of pacing the meeting appropriately to ensure that the meeting objectives are honored. It does not mean that every agenda item ends exactly as scheduled, but it does mean that presenters are kept on topic so the meeting value is not hijacked. Essentially, flow involves keeping your meeting focused on the objectives and agenda and on time.

Managing Agenda Topics

A key aspect of managing the meeting flow is effectively transitioning from one agenda item to the next and maintaining momentum in the process. Once you've initiated your meeting, the first place to start, obviously, is with your first agenda item. A general framework for transitioning to an agenda item and maintaining flow is to:

(a) call out the agenda item

(b) introduce the agenda leader

(c) remind the topic leader (and other attendees) how much time is allocated to their topics

> *Example: All right, so I'm going to pass it over to Bryan to kick us off. Bryan is going to provide us with an overview of the databases the hacker was able to access and how we believe he/she was successful. Bryan, we have you on the agenda for twenty minutes.*

Informing a stakeholder how much time he has is no guarantee that he will stay within budget, but it most certainly helps. It also sets an expectation that time matters, and that you will cut in if he consumes too much of it. In instances where you're working with an agenda leader who is a notorious time offender, consider a tactic of providing time warnings throughout their presentation.

> *Example: I'm going to pass it over to Bryan to kick us off. Bryan is going to provide us with an overview of the databases the hacker was able to access and how we believe he/she was successful. Bryan, we have you on the agenda for twenty minutes. I'll give you a five-minute warning to make sure we have time for questions.*

While this might seem like a subtle difference, it's proven to be effective in managing flow.

Managing Attendee Focus

Another key aspect of meeting flow is to keep attendees engaged and focused on the meeting objectives. It is inevitable that someone in your meeting will introduce a discussion that has little or nothing to do with the objectives of the meeting.

Managing flow does not mean that you cut these people (and their comments) off. We all know that sometimes it's the boss who is a key offender for staying on track. What it does mean is that the meeting leader needs to be sensitive to dialogue that is off topic and professionally align everyone back to the task at hand.

We'll discuss how to do this in chapter six, "Meeting Skills and Tools," but for now it's important to understand that the meeting leader is responsible for flow and for continually directing attendees back to the scope of the meeting (i.e. the objectives and agenda).

Capture

Beyond the meeting flow, the most important responsibility of the meeting manager is to make sure that the important information that surfaced in the meeting is captured. With PSM we refer to this information as "meeting assets"

The importance of capturing meeting assets is so critical that we've dedicated an entire chapter (five) to the rationale and mechanics for collecting this information. For now it's important to note it is the meeting manager's responsibility (or in some instances a designee) to capture this intellectual property that is generated throughout each agenda item discussion. Meeting assets represent the essential distinctions raised during the course of your meetings. These include items such as decisions, action item assignments, issues identified and other key ideas or concepts.

The PSM system relies on the capturing and communication of meeting assets as a cornerstone strategy for mitigating each of the five meeting killers raised in chapter two.

Keep in mind that the meeting manager does not own all the meeting assets raised during the course of a meeting, but he or she does maintain the responsibility to ensure they are captured so that they can be clarified and shared with key stakeholders and leveraged in the future.

Meeting Conclusion

The final step in the body of the meeting execution phase is to bring the meeting to conclusion. A common tendency of meeting managers is to allow meetings to run until the end of the allocated time without leaving time for necessary summary and closure. As a result, meetings frequently run over or end abruptly as attendees hustle off to other obligations.

For a standard one-hour meeting a meeting manager should begin concluding with approximately five to ten minutes left in the meeting. This is important for several reasons:

1. It provides time to communicate and clarify meeting assets (when needed) and discuss next steps.

2. It minimizes the need for follow-up meetings if you leave enough time to complete necessary discussion or decision.

3. It guards against "backloading" where attendees introduce a last-minute curveball topic at the end of a meeting with no time to discuss.

Concluding the meeting is as simple as reviewing the key assets captured throughout the meeting and confirming next steps and expectations.

Remember that a key focus of PSM is to reinforce clarity and accountability of meeting content. You cannot assume that all meeting attendees heard the same things and came to the same conclusions. It is better to assume that everyone in the meeting did not hear the same things and allow time for a brief review and any necessary clarifications.

It is also important to keep in mind that it is common to uncover disagreement when recapping meeting assets and concluding a meeting. This might require you to reopen some of the discussion to ensure attendees are aligned. This is actually a good thing! It's better to surface the disagreement while everyone is still assembled, than having to deal with it later. The point of concluding the meeting appropriately is to ensure that attendees are aligned as they exit the meeting. However even the most skilled meeting manager cannot guarantee that everyone gets completely aligned, and remains aligned. Which brings us to the next phase of meeting execution—reporting.

Reporting

A crank is someone with a new idea—until it catches on.

—Mark Twain

We recently participated in a half-day collaborative meeting with the CEO and her senior team at a multibillion-dollar, international corporation. The objective of the session was to obtain senior executive alignment and vital input into the company's highest priority business initiative.

Throughout the four-hour meeting many valuable distinctions were made. Decisions on how to move the business forward, commitments to take action by members of the senior team, worthy ideas about the evolution of the business and significant issues with the current operating structure that were inhibiting progress.

Throughout the discussion, meeting assets were identified and captured. At times we would interject to clarify comments or decisions and other times the outcome was self-evident. Shortly after the meeting adjourned, we distributed a meeting summary report (that is, a synopsis of the key decisions, ideas, action commitments and identified issues to the members of the team.) We then asked the executive team to review and comment to be sure that we had a common understanding of the important meeting points.

Soon after the meeting we received a thank-you email from the chief operating officer (COO) of this organization noting:

> *Thank you for the clear and concise follow up. I've been around for a while and this is the first time we've circulated our decisions and commitments. Much needed and appreciated.*

We simply captured the essential elements (that is, key points, decisions, commitments) of their meeting discussion and sent it back to them in a timely manner. However the impact to the clarity of their outcomes and the associated accountability was significant and unprecedented.

The reporting phase of PSM is straightforward, yet critical to ensuring clarity, accountability and follow-through. In our experience we've observed meeting output taking one of two main forms: meeting minutes or nothing, with the vast majority of meeting output being nothing. It's hard to fathom how so many organizations spend so much time in critical collaborative meetings without documented meeting output.

While producing meeting minutes is typically better than doing nothing, minutes tend to be too bulky and fail to distinguish important information from superfluous content. Readers are left to fend for themselves to sift the meeting wheat from the chaff. This approach does little to improve the clarity and accountability we desperately need in the meeting process. To make matters worse, meeting minutes take a lot of time to prepare and are rarely ever read.

The PSM results phase culminates with the distribution of a meeting summary report that captures the most important meeting assets and a few pieces of other important information.

Key principles for the meeting results phase include preparing and distributing a meeting summary report that includes the following components.

Visit http://meetingresult.com/psmmember to download a complimentary meeting summary report template for your use.

- Meeting Assets—Document all the meeting assets captured and the relevant details (description, dates, owner, et cetera).

- Meeting Objective Review —Confirm whether the meeting objective was accomplished.

- Agenda Items Covered—Identify the agenda items that were completed and those that were not completed, noting the leader of each agenda item.

- Meeting Attendees—Document who attended and who didn't.

- Meeting Logistics—Date, time, duration, (for reference purposes).

- Other Messages—Any additional messages that should be shared with the team related to the meeting (for example, next meeting date, thank you, et cetera).

We recommend that the meeting leader distribute the meeting summary report within forty-eight hours after the meeting occurred (within twenty-four hours is ideal). Quick turnaround is necessary to reinforce accountability and obtain feedback while the content is fresh in attendees' minds. This also demonstrates the importance of the meeting and attendee time by distributing the summary in a timely manner. Ultimately, prompt distribution ensures that everyone is on the same page and significantly reduces the possibility of misalignment.

Stakeholders should be asked to review the meeting summary report and comment/edit as needed. This provides attendees an opportunity to comment and adds to their ownership of the meeting outcomes. It also gives attendees an opportunity to reconfirm the key points of the meeting before it is memorialized.

Once any feedback is received, the last step is to distribute the final version of the meeting summary report to the stakeholders and subscribers. This ensures that subscribers have the information they need to perform their role and provides a clean starting point for your next meeting.

Throughout the reporting process and the entire PSM system, the cornerstone of effectiveness rests with the identification, capture and communication of meeting assets—a topic we'll tackle next.

As a reminder, PSM readers get an exclusive offer to try our Web-based meeting management software. The software automates the PSM process of building agendas, capturing meeting assets, and creating meeting summary reports. Just go to http://meetingresult.com/psmmember to learn more.

5 MEETING ASSETS

Complex is easy. Simple is hard. Simplicity needs a champion.

—Ken Segall

As outlined in chapter four, meeting assets represent the fruit of your business meetings. They are a collection of the intellectual property produced during the course of your meetings: important ideas, distinctions, actions, and decisions. Learning how to identify, extract and communicate meeting assets is the cornerstone of the PSM system. If your only takeaway from this book is learning how to effectively manage meeting assets, then you will still significantly improve the quality of your business meetings.

How often do you attend meetings where ideas are expressed, plans are being sketched, options are being explored, decisions are being made and action items are being vetted? All the time, right? How often do those meetings end with all those ideas, plans, decisions and action items seemingly left in the middle of the conference room table?

Of course attendees take notes or rely on their memories to recall the information previously discussed in their meetings, but how reliable is that? Have you ever been in a meeting with the same attendees discussing the same topic all over again? Of course you have, and you probably have thought to yourself, *what a waste of time!*

If meeting objectives represent a vacation destination, then meeting assets are the memories that are made along the way. Like taking a camera on vacation to capture the most important memories, the PSM system captures the most vital meeting distinctions to ensure they can be utilized.

The Asset Mindset

Even as you read this book, there are likely multiple stimuli vying for your attention. There might be a television or music playing in the background, a conversation occurring in a nearby room, an ache in your lower back, or random thoughts crossing your mind. Fortunately, our brains have a mechanism that allows us to filter common distractions so we can focus on a specific task. Without this filter our individual productivity would be dreadful.

With competing opinions, personalities and diversions, meetings create a unique filtering challenge for the meeting leader. The meeting environment and its subsequent "noise" produce a climate that breeds the meeting killers we introduced in chapter two—particularly high ambiguity, limited accountability, insufficient data and inadequate process. Outstanding meeting leaders know how to minimize this noise and extract the intellectual property generated. A meeting asset mindset enables meeting leaders to filter out the distractions in the meeting environment and focus on the valuable intellectual property that is created.

Once your brain is focused on collecting meeting assets, you will realize just how prevalent they are within your meeting space. Even in the least productive meetings, meeting assets are sure to exist. The PSM system trains your brain to identify these assets and provides a process to generate even more of them.

Have you ever noticed when you're in the market for a specific type of vehicle you tend to see those vehicles everywhere? Coincidence? Of course not. Your brain focuses on (and finds more of) whatever is top of your mind. That's exactly how meeting assets work once you know what you're looking for.

The Asset Model

Specific meeting assets can vary depending on the context of the meeting. A project-based meeting might have assets that identify action items, decisions, issues, key notes and risks. A sales meeting might have assets that identify objections, competitor intelligence, key assumptions, client commitments and more. Regardless of the business context, meeting assets surface in every collaborative meeting. It is the meeting leader's responsibility to ensure the assets are identified, clarified and documented.

Prepare

Meeting managers must have the capability to focus on the meeting content and capture the intellectual property that is being created throughout the meeting management process. This capability comes through building skills and awareness that allow meeting managers to effectively assess the meeting content.

The first step is to identify the assets you are looking to extract from your meetings. This involves thinking through the underlying business process and brainstorming through a few key questions.

- What types of outcomes from my meetings are important to document?

- What expertise should be extracted from my meeting attendees?

- What type of information should be shared with my meeting subscribers?

- What types of assignments or tasks commonly surface in my meetings?

- What types of meeting discussion has caused problems in the past due to a lack of clarity?

Take a moment to go through each of these questions and write down your thoughts. You should begin to see some patterns emerge on the most essential content produced in your meetings. These are your meeting assets.

To assist you, we've created a complimentary tool to help you identify your meeting assets. Go to http://meetingresult.com/psmmember to access the asset identification tool.

Figure 5.1 provides some examples of meeting assets for various types of meetings.

Our discussion will focus on the project-based meeting assets that include action items, decisions, key ideas/notes, issues and risks.

Figure 5.1. Assets for Different Meeting Types

Once you have determined your meeting assets, the next step is understanding the attributes related to each asset. For example, let's consider the following action item.

Notify Finance that additional funding will be needed for the data center expansion.

This action items requires a couple of attributes to be clear and useful. One to clarify ownership (that is, who is going to take the action) and one to clarify when the action item needs to be completed (that is, due date). Remember, clarity is key. Even relatively skilled meeting leaders can fail to capture the attributes that allow us to fully comprehend and utilize an asset. Figure 5.2 provides an example of asset attributes for a project-based meeting.

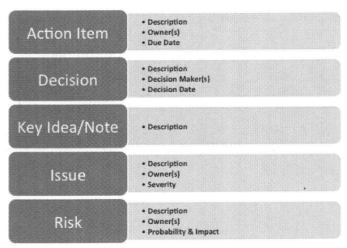

Figure 5.2. Project-Based Meeting Assets

Take a moment to think through the required attributes for each of your meeting assets. When you've got a good list of assets and attributes take some time to vet this list with some colleagues (that is, meeting attendees and subscribers) and incorporate their ideas. Once complete you'll have a baseline meeting asset model.

With your asset model set, the final preparation is to communicate your approach to your meeting attendees. Let them know that your goal is to make your time together as productive as possible and that you will be capturing and clarifying the assets of the meeting and communicating them back to ensure that everyone is on the same page. You are also setting expectations for the attendees about generating assets throughout the course of the meeting agenda and dialogue.

Capture

Once you know what you are looking for, capturing meeting assets is a fairly straightforward process. The objective is simple, cut through the meeting noise and capture assets and their attributes as they arise. The key is for meeting managers to remain focused on the strategic content in the meeting and ignore the superfluous conversation.

Capturing meeting assets involves four key components to be performed during your meeting:

1. Identify—The most obvious step is to identify that an asset has surfaced during your meeting. This task becomes much simpler now that you have a clear asset model in place.

2. Clarify—Meeting assets are often raised with some degree of ambiguity either on the overall intent (for example, did we just make a final decision or are we still debating this matter?) or in the attributes of the asset (for example, owner or date). An example of this would be an action item that's raised without an owner or a due date.

    So HR is going to prepare the draft proposal and send it to Rhonda and Tom.

    There's obviously some important information that the meeting leader needs to clarify. This includes **who** in HR is preparing the draft proposal and **when** it will be sent to Rhonda and Tom.

3. Document—Meeting assets that have been identified and clarified are relatively useless unless they are documented for future communication and reinforcement.

4. Tag—as mentioned in chapter four, tagging is about informing key stakeholders who might not be in the meeting but might need to be

informed of certain meeting content. Once an asset has been documented, the next step is to identify anyone else who needs to be aware of this specific information. In our example above, Rhonda and Tom might need to be tagged so they are aware that the draft proposal is coming their way.

These steps require the meeting manager to possess the capability to identify meeting assets, capture the relevant data associated with the assets and ensure they are assigned to the appropriate owner (if applicable).

Sometimes this requires meeting managers to stop the flow of the meeting and make certain that the assets are captured properly. Asking people to repeat or summarize a statement is often necessary and useful because it reinforces what is being said and documented. This is especially true with meeting assets such as action items or decisions where clarification and accountability are especially important.

However, it is not always possible or practical to interrupt the meeting flow and verbally repeat every meeting asset at the time they surface. Meeting leaders need to use good judgment to determine when to interject and when to take a note for later follow up. Keep in mind that PSM provides multiple opportunities to clarify your meeting assets.

If you're interested in a streamlined way to capture meeting assets, check out MeetingResult's Web-based software. It's easy to use and PSM readers are eligible for an exclusive offer.

Visit http://meetingresult.com/psmmember to learn more.

Communicate

Some assets must be clarified immediately (for example, the rest of the meeting hinges on the clarity of a decision) in order to move forward. In this case the need to immediately interject and clarify is obvious.

Others assets need to be clarified before the meeting is ended and attendees leave, but can wait until the conclusion section of the meeting. In chapter four we discussed the final step in the body of the meeting execution phase is to bring the meeting to conclusion. An essential step in the process is to summarize and clarify meeting assets as needed.

Still others assets (particularly non-action oriented assets, such as key notes) can often be reviewed and clarified after the meeting has ended as part of the meeting summary report process.

At the conclusion of each meeting, a summary of the meeting results and the captured assets should be documented and communicated to each meeting stakeholder and subscriber. As mentioned in chapter four it is important to note that a meeting summary report does not equal meeting minutes. A meeting summary report is limited to the most important highlights so that all attendees and other key stakeholders can quickly review the outcomes and clarify if needed.

Meeting Assets Summary

Meeting assets are the single most important defense for battling the five meeting killers. When effectively utilized they bring clarity to your meetings by clearly documenting key points and their associated attributes (who, what, when). Meeting assets contribute to increased accountability by ensuring that each attendee knows what is expected of them, and by making those expectations clear to others. Capturing meeting assets also provides essential data on the meeting outcomes.

Finally, meeting assets help to combat the problem of over attendance in meetings. Meeting leaders who effectively capture and communicate meeting assets provide the appropriate highlights to interested but non-essential stakeholders (that is, subscribers) who can review the information in a fraction of the time it would take to attend the entire meeting.

Remember to visit us at
http://meetingresult.com/psmmember for additional
resources and exclusive offers.

6 MEETING SKILLS & TOOLS

Habit is the intersection of knowledge (what to do), skill (how to do), and desire (want to do).

—Stephen R. Covey

While good process is the cornerstone of conducting effective business meetings and the first defense against the five meeting killers, a skilled leader is required to effectively operate the process. Just as the fastest racecar requires a talented driver to navigate the racetrack, a good meeting process is dependent on a capable leader to drive at the highest levels of efficiency and effectiveness. In our experience, there are four essential skills that great meeting leaders must possess to drive the powerfully simple meeting (PSM) system.

#1 Listening

The capacity to be an excellent listener is fundamental to leading great meetings. Managing meeting flow and the collection of assets hinges on the capability of the meeting leader to be fully attentive.

Have you ever attended a meeting where the meeting leader is noticeably distracted and mentally absent?

This person might be physically present but her mind is in a faraway place. Like riding a bus with a texting bus driver, a distracted meeting leader is a danger to our meeting effectiveness.

When most people think of listening, they think of an instinctive human function (such as breathing or blinking) that requires little conscious thought or training. But nothing could be further from the truth. With hectic professional lives filled by enormous levels of distraction, the quality of our listening is inversely related to the amount of distraction we are experiencing at any point in time.

Fortunately, listening is an active process that can be strengthened and conditioned. And it is essential for great meeting management. As a meeting leader you must be prepared to minimize your distraction and fully listen in any meeting that you are leading.

As you leverage PSM and grow in your meeting management capability, our objective here is to raise your awareness of your listening capacity and its importance in effective meeting management. As you read further we ask that you reflect on your listening skills and assess how you're showing up in your business meetings.

We have identified two listening "zones" that meeting leaders find themselves in during the course of a meeting, the *zone of distraction* and the *zone of focus*.

Zone of Distraction

The zone of distraction is when you are physically present in the meeting, but mentally you are in a different place. This zone occurs anytime your attention drifts to anything other than:

- Meeting attendees

- Meeting objectives and agenda

- Meeting process

- Content of the meeting (for example, meeting assets)

Some meeting leaders might fall into this distraction zone for just a few moments, others might spend an entire meeting in this space. This zone results from your focus being diverted to another external stimulus or your own internal dialogue.

Examples of external stimulus include email, texts, phone calls or sidebar meeting conversations. They are things in the environment that draw your attention away from the content of the meeting and to another place. We all get the urge to check our phones every now and again to see if we've received an important email, text or phone call. That might just be a way of life for most of us, but a meeting leader cannot succumb to the lures of this external distraction.

We can also get caught up on our own internal conversation. This is a preoccupation with your thoughts or emotions. In this instance you might actually be looking directly at a meeting attendee who is speaking while nodding your head. But in reality you're not really "hearing" a word that he is saying. You might be thinking about a personal matter, other work that you need to perform, or just considering what you want to say next. In either case, it is easy for our attention to wander away from the content of the meeting if we are not *actively* listening.

Meeting managers must consciously maintain a focus on the meeting, the content and the needs of attendees to avoid the zone of distraction. The first step is to be aware of your tendencies. Recognize when you slip out of focus and immediately shift your focus back to your meeting attendees, objectives, agenda and content—back to the zone of focus.

Zone of Focus

The zone of focus means that you are fully engaged in the meeting dialogue. Your focus and attention is on the meeting objectives, attendees, process and the corresponding discussion. You are listening to what attendees are saying and how they are saying it. You are interpreting their body language, hearing their tones and consciously soaking it all in.

While you are listening, you are also acutely aware of the group dynamic. You can sense when others are paying attention and assess if attendees are confused, have a question or want to comment.

When you are in this zone of focus, you are able to effectively sift important content from extraneous dialogue. You can more clearly perform your role and clarify essential assets generated throughout the meeting. Further, your attentiveness in this zone influences attendees to maintain their focus and engagement. When meeting leaders check out of the discussion others are sure to follow. Fortunately the opposite is also true.

In this space you resist the temptation to respond to the external or internal distractions that are sure to present themselves throughout the meeting.

Simply stated, maintaining attentive listening is a critical responsibility of the meeting leader. With focused listening a meeting leader is in a powerful position to impact the quality of meeting results—especially when listening is supplemented with the skill of asking great questions.

#2 Questioning

One of the single most important tools of any leader or communicator is the ability to ask good questions. A good question can refocus a conversation, expand our thinking and clarify uncertainties. In a meeting context, good questions are the most important tool in obtaining clarity, alignment and accountability.

Questions can take on various forms and be used for many purposes. Within the meeting context we identify three types of questions as paramount. As you read the descriptions below, you might realize that you are already leveraging these types of questions in your daily work. Our objective is to raise your awareness so you can use them more intentionally to drive the results you desire in your meetings.

Close-Ended Questions

Close-ended questions are designed to generate a focused response, such as "yes" or "no," or option A, B or C. These questions limit the choice of responses, eliminate ambiguity and are a vital tool for every meeting manager to make important distinctions. For example: *Are you confirming that the system will be ready for user acceptance testing by October 1, 2014?*

It is possible that someone might answer this question with a lengthy response explaining all of the challenges of the project, but the bottom line is ultimately going to be yes or no.

Close-ended questions cut right to the chase and should be used intentionally to confirm or deny a meeting outcome. Consider this example: *Would everyone agree that we've made a decision to delay the project until February 1?* This question warrants a yes or no response. Anything else means that you have more work to do in order to get the clarity you need.

Close-ended questions provide a clear response without consuming too much meeting time. They are simple and efficient questions for confirming alignment. However, there are times when you need to elicit more information and open up the dialogue to surface more context. In this case you need to move to an open-ended question.

Open-Ended Questions

Open-ended questions require more than a simple yes or no answer. They are exploratory questions designed to dig beneath the surface of the discussion. Open-ended questions facilitate the gathering and sharing of information during the meeting process.

Unlike responses to close-ended questions, open-ended questions can consume a lot of meeting time as the individual responds. Some of this information might be valuable and some might not.

An example of an open-ended question is: *Would you share your thoughts on the decision to delay the project until February?*

If you're looking for confirmation or clarification, then a close-ended question is more suitable. If you are interested in exploring ideas, opportunities and risks, then open-ended questions are the way to go.

Consider another open-ended question used in a situation where a stakeholder is struggling with the option of postponing a project: *What are some alternatives to postponing the project until February?* This might or might not surface other ideas or support the stakeholder in their thinking process. It will, however, generate more possibilities than a close-ended question.

Regardless of the questions asked, the importance is for meeting managers to be intentional with their questions, and think through the type of response they are seeking.

Specifying Questions

Somewhere in between close-ended and open-ended questions rests a type of question we refer to as a *specifying question*. Specifying questions do not provide a finite list of options (for example, yes or no), and they are not open to whatever thoughts or feelings a stakeholder wants to express (that is, open-ended questions). Specifying questions are designed to help attendees make specific statements in a timely manner.

Our model of specifying questioning is adapted from Neuro Linguistic Programming's (NLP) Meta Model developed by Richard Bandler and Dr. John Grinder. It provides powerful tools for creating clearer, more-precise meeting communication. Specifying questions provide the tools needed to bring clarity to meeting dialogue.

Verbal communications that occur within meetings cannot reasonably include all contextual detail; there is not enough time for stakeholders to articulate every thought. In the interest of time, attendees will unconsciously filter (that is, delete or simplify) their language in order to express their thoughts. Stakeholders try to be specific enough to get the desired results, and at the same time, eliminate extraneous information. Though sometimes the "extraneous" information they delete is actually essential to obtain the clarity we need.

Great meeting leaders know when to ask a specifying question to obtain the precision needed. In a meeting context we focus on specifying questions in three primary instances. Unspecified nouns, actions and timing. While there are multiple ways to dig for clarity in each instance, we propose a simple model that includes an interrogative pronoun (that is, who, what, how, when) followed by the word "specifically." Here are some examples of the context and the specifying question:

Unspecified Nouns

An unspecified noun is a person, place or thing that is unclear in the stakeholder's communication. For example: "OK, I'll have them set it up and have that over to you later next week." It is not entirely clear who "them" is and what "it" is. Meeting leaders need to determine the importance of any missing information and obtain it.

To remedy this, the question could be: "*Who specifically* is going to set it up?" Another important question could be, "*What specifically* are they setting up?" When you recognize these unspecified nouns you must determine if the missing information is important, and if so, get it.

Unspecified Action

Another area of ambiguity comes in the form of action. An unspecified action is a verb that is especially vague. For example: "My team will knock it out next week." Perhaps you know what they mean by "knock it out" or you might want to clarify by responding, "*How specifically* are you going to knock it out?"

Consider another example: "We'll have the training room ready to go when the executive team arrives next week." Again, you might know what "ready" means or you might need to clarify by asking, "*How specifically* will it be ready?"

It is not suggested that you need to bring specificity questions to every ambiguous term that arises in a meeting. The point is for meeting managers to recognize ambiguity and remove it whenever necessary.

Unspecified Timing

When it comes to enforcing accountability, it is not uncommon for attendees to dodge being pinned down to a specific date for completing their work. There are times when it is not feasible or practical to determine an exact date or time to complete a deliverable. Yet there is a significant opportunity to improve our clarity in this area using specifying questions.

As career project managers, we have made a living from specifying nebulous deliverable dates for tasks and action items. We have also heard every ambiguous term imaginable. Our personal favorite is when a delivery "date" encompasses an entire season. Such as, "we should have that done by the summer." Talk about wiggle room! That might be acceptable in some circumstances, but where it is not, meeting leaders need to respond accordingly.

Unspecified timing is simply a situation where the meeting attendee leaves the date or time of a task, deliverable or event, unclear or unstated. For example: "We should have that done by the summer." If needed, the ready response to this is, "*When specifically* in the summer do you estimate having that done?"

Specifying questions are a simple, effective tool for obtaining clarification.

If you want to go further into mastering this meeting leader skill, we've got a great training video for you at this link: http://meetingresult.com/psmmember.

#3 Redirecting

Keeping attendees focused on producing results consistent with a meeting's objectives and agenda is a vital responsibility of a meeting leader. This task can become challenging depending on the nature of the meeting content, attendee personalities and the natural inclination for stakeholders to veer off topic.

Consider an airplane flying from New York to Los Angeles. During the course of the five-hour flight, an airplane is continually flying off course. Winds aloft are pushing the aircraft in different directions requiring the pilot to make regular adjustments to keep the plane on the proper heading. The role of the plane's navigational systems is to provide timely information that the pilot can use to make needed adjustments to keep the airplane flying on a course that minimizes travel time, maximizes fuel efficiency and ensures arrival at the correct destination.

Like airplanes, meetings have an inherent tendency to travel off course. Without a capable navigation system (that is, PSM) and pilot (that is, meeting leader), our meetings risk ending up at the wrong destination or crashing into a sea of directionless inefficiency. This can happen when stakeholders innocently steer meetings in the wrong direction (that is, away from achieving our meeting objectives) or worse, when they deliberately attempt to hijack.

Chapter four describes the tools and process we can leverage to act as our navigation system (for example, establishing meeting objectives, agendas), but we also need a skilled pilot to ensure that our meetings remain on course. Leveraging a skill we refer to as *redirecting*.

Redirecting is about getting meeting attendees back on track when they stray from the focus of the meeting. As it is virtually impossible to keep meeting attendees on course all the time, a meeting leader must be skilled enough to bring everyone back on track when needed. Redirecting requires:

- Awareness of when a meeting is heading off course.

- Patience to allow a reasonable amount of time for wayward attendees to get themselves back on track.

- Action when needed to get the meeting back on track.

The first step in keeping meeting attendees on track is knowing that they are off course if the first place. This awareness comes from a meeting leader having a clear understanding of the meeting objectives and agenda (chapter four), and remaining in the listening *zone of focus* (discussed earlier in this chapter). An inattentive meeting leader without a clear understanding of the meeting objectives has little hope of efficiently leading attendees to their destination.

Second, meeting leaders need to be calculated in redirecting attendees' focus. A meeting leader that regularly redirects too quickly can alienate attendees by squelching their creative thinking and might be perceived as an overbearing control freak. Attendees demand some wiggle room to stray off course and often times will get themselves back on track. However once it becomes clear that attendees have lost their way, meeting leaders cannot just sit idly by and watch time being wasted with irrelevant, stagnant or belabored discussion.

Unfortunately there are no hard rules about exactly when to redirect attendees. This must be left to the judgment of the meeting leader in consideration of a host of environmental factors (for example, the individual or individuals who are leading the meeting off course, the other attendees involved, time constraints, meeting content, cultural norms, politics). However once it's determined that the meeting is straying too far off course, it's time for the meeting leader to take corrective action.

Our focus for the remainder of this section will center on the specific actions that meeting leaders can take to redirect meeting attendees to get their meetings back on track.

Pre-Frame

The first tactic for redirecting attendees happens before the need to redirect ever surfaces, a tactic we call the *pre-frame*. The pre-frame establishes the expectation that attendees stay on target and that the meeting leader will take the responsibility for keeping the meeting on track. This is best performed during the initiation phase of the meeting or in advance of the meeting if you are managing a meeting that is at high risk of going off course.

Example: Before reviewing our agenda I want to mention that we have an aggressive schedule and are very tight on time. So it's important that we stay on topic. If it looks as if we're heading off course from our objectives. I'm asking your permission to get us back on track. Does that work for everyone?

In this pre-frame example the meeting leader sets the expectation for staying on track and asks for permission to redirect the team as needed. What is the likelihood that attendees would object to someone keeping them on track? The important point here is to prepare attendees for the potential redirect in advance. While this tactic is not foolproof, it does increase the likelihood that attendees will stay on track and greases the skids for redirecting them when they don't.

We recently managed a strategic planning offsite meeting for a Fortune 500 organization. The meeting included several of the top senior executives in the company (traditionally not the easiest stakeholders to redirect) and was at high risk of getting off course due to the strong opinions represented and the contentiousness of the meeting content. Prior to the meeting we paid special attention to pre-framing the need to stay on task in each communication leading up to the meeting in addition to during personal conversations with each attendee.

The results of the pre-frame tactic were simply outstanding. Attendees remained mostly on track and even when they didn't, they generally acknowledged to the team that they were intentionally going a little off topic but to "please hear them out." During nearly eight hours of elapsed meeting time, the team needed no more than four redirects to keep everyone on track. As a result the meeting successfully ended on time with all agenda items completed and all objective accomplished.

With the pre-frame groundwork established let's review the four specific tactics you can leverage to get your meeting back on track.

1. Hard Redirect

A hard redirect is the most simple and efficient way to get your meeting attendees back on track. However because it is so direct, it might not be appropriate in every organizational culture.

Meeting Leader: *OK, we're getting off course, as this discussion is not directly related to our meeting objectives. In the interest of everyone's time, we need to move forward.*

The approach here is simple and direct:

(a) Interrupt the wayward discussion.

(b) Explain why it's important to get on track (that is, for the sake of time).

(c) Tell attendees where to go next.

The hard redirect is short but not so sweet, which is why sometimes a softer redirect is in order.

2. Soft Redirect

The soft redirect follows a similar syntax to the hard redirect but is done in a more sensitive manner. The soft redirect is more appropriate for organization cultures and meeting environments where ruffling feathers is not welcomed.

Meeting Leader: *OK I appreciate where you're going with this discussion, and I also know that we're getting away from the meeting objectives we established. So in respect of our time together I suggest we move forward.*

The approach here is similar to the hard redirect but is done in a slightly more elegant way:

(a) Interrupt the wayward discussion by *"appreciating"* their thoughts *"and"* letting them know that *"we're"* straying from the agenda.

(b) Explain why it's important to get on track.

(c) "Suggest" then where to go next and move on.

The approach here is similar to the hard redirect with some noticeable differences in language choice. In particular please note the use of the words *appreciate, and,* and *we're* in step (a) above. These words are used intentionally to get attendees back on track in a more collegial manner.

3. Segue

Occasionally meeting attendees will get entrenched in an area of dialogue that just isn't going any further. Meeting attendees aren't necessarily off track, but the discussion has clearly exhausted itself and there really isn't any more ground to cover. This can happen in places of violent agreement where attendees continually reinforce each other, or instances where they just get lost reflecting on and rehashing the recent dialogue. In any case the path forward here is a simple tactic we refer to as the segue.

Meeting Leader: *OK, well done, and that's a great segue to our next agenda item.*

The segue provides a clean (friendly) transition point for attendees while acknowledging the progress that's been made.

(a) Interrupt the exhausted discussion.

(b) Acknowledge the progress made (for example, "well done").

(c) Segue to the next agenda item.

The approach here is so simple and yet it's a remarkably effective tool for moving meetings along in a very efficient manner.

4. Capture and Move On

It is common to reach an area of discussion that is well within the scope of the meeting (that is, it is not off topic) yet is far from being complete (that is, not something to segue). These discussions happen when there is an impasse or a stalemate that has been reached and it's clear that it's not going to be resolved during the meeting time allocated. Rather than consuming precious meeting time, the role of the meeting leader is to redirect in a way that doesn't ignore the impasse but allows the meeting to continue—a tactic we refer to as capture and move on.

Meeting Leader: *OK, it's clear we're not going to solve this issue during our time today, and I want to be sure we use our time wisely, so I will capture this as an open item and ensure we have enough time allocated in our next meeting to resolve. So let's move on.*

The goal is to bring the discussion to a close so that it can be addressed at a more optimal time (that is, when you have sufficient time and attendance to resolve the matter). Like all the other redirect tactics, the first step is to interrupt the discussion, followed by three steps that allow for a quick transition back to your meeting:

(a) Interrupt the stalled discussion.

(b) Explain why it's important to table the discussion (for example, in the interest of time).

(c) Ensure attendees that the matter will be captured.

(d) Assign (or take) an action item to do whatever needs to be done next.

Attendees need closure on open items and want to know that some action is going to be taken as a result of the discussion. Capture and move on provides them what they want so that you can productively move forward with the rest of your meeting.

If you want to go further into mastering this meeting leader skill, we've got a great training video for you at this link: <u>http://meetingresult.com/psmmember</u>.

#4 Summarizing

Summarizing is a skill that is rarely found in a resume or listed in a job description. It is not taught in business school or corporate training programs, but summarizing is a critical skill when it comes to meeting management. The ability to take a large sum of information and distill it (that is, clarify) into key themes, concepts, thoughts and ideas is essential.

As with other meeting skills we have discussed, summarizing has broader applicability beyond just meeting management. Learning clearer, more concise communication skills is a benefit in virtually any situation. The key to making a great pasta sauce is to slowly cook the sauce during a period of several hours to reduce the amount of water, which enhances the flavors of the tomatoes and spices. The more filler we remove from our communications to make them more concise, the clearer and better our communications become.

Comment Summarizing

Comment summarizing takes place at an individual stakeholder level to ensure attendees have correctly understood what the stakeholder means to communicate. Throughout the course of a meeting, it is common for stakeholders to think out loud when expressing an opinion, thought or idea. They might not hear what they have actually said. They just say it. Comment summarizing allows the meeting manager to ensure the stakeholder actually hears what they have just said. This provides stakeholders the opportunity to confirm their intent and edit themselves if necessary.

Comment summarization extracts the extraneous information and plays back the parts that are most relevant to the content of the meeting. It also provides the space to obtain the necessary clarity we have emphasized throughout this book. The following is an example of comment summarization:

Meeting Manager: *What are your recommendations on how to proceed with the systems upgrade project?*

Attendee 1: *I think we need to delay the initiation of the project. Until we know the final budget, it would be a waste of time to start a project only to have it cancelled a month later. We did that last year with the CRM system and it was a tremendous waste of my time and my team's time, and we're already way over capacity thanks to staffing cuts. Besides, there's no real risk of being unsupported by the vendor for a few months. The technology platform has been stable and we have a great relationship with the vendor if we run into a crisis.*

Meeting Manager (comment summary): *OK. So you're recommendation is to delay the upgrade project until the budget is confirmed, due to the risk of wasting resource time when there's no real risk of being unsupported by the vendor.*

Attendee 1: *Well, there's not exactly no risk. There is some risk with being unsupported. It's just not as great as everyone is making it out to be. Perhaps the best way to handle this is to perform a formal risk assessment and then make the decision whether or not to initiate the project now.*

In this case the summary enabled the attendee to actually hear what she was saying. If the meeting manager had not performed the comment summary, attendees would have heard that there was *no risk* to delaying the project. Playing back the statement clarified a measure of risk that should be assessed.

Meeting managers might hesitate to perform a comment summary for fear of coming across as confrontational or aloof, but it is important to remember that clarity is key. Comment summarizing is a direct component of staying in the zone of focus.

The true skill resides in knowing when and how to appropriately apply this summarizing concept. It is the meeting manager's responsibility to identify the ideas, thoughts and opinions that require validation or clarity. As a general rule when you identify something as a meeting asset you should use summarizing to make sure clarity is achieved.

Conversational Summarizing

Have you ever met someone who can recount a twenty-minute conversation nearly sentence-by-sentence without losing much detail? It takes skill to recount an experience or a conversation and describe seemingly every word spoken, and how it was spoken. Being an attentive listener certainly contributes to this skill.

Even more impressive are the people who can take a twenty-minute conversation and boil it down to a two-minute recap without compromising the true meaning, spirit and flavor of the conversation. These people know how to tell the story, provide the important highlights and move forward. They are great conversational summarizers.

Conversational summarizing might happen at various points within a meeting. It is more an art than a science, and there is no exact formula of when to summarize a conversation. A general rule is that a conversational summary should occur after each significant agenda item or collection of each significant asset. Continuing with our example from above:

Attendee 2: *If we take too long to get the upgrade initiated, we will not be able to complete it on time. To me that is the bigger risk—to just keep talking, analyzing it and not take any action.*

Attendee 1: *I don't mind taking action as long as we're not wasting my team's time.*

Attendee 3: *Performing the planning phase activities or the upgrade will not consume too many resources and the documentation can be leveraged in the future—even if we decide to delay.*

Attendee 2: *My team can support some of the planning activities for a couple of weeks while your team performs the risk assessment in support of a final decision.*

Meeting Manager: *When can you have the risk assessment completed?*

Attendee 1: *Probably a couple of weeks.*

Meeting Manager: *Can you commit to having it completed by our next meeting, June 14th, so we can make a decision at that time?*

Attendee 1: *That will work.*

Meeting Manager: *Does that work for everyone else?*

All: *Yes.*

Meeting Manager (conversational summary): *So let me summarize what we just discussed to make sure we are all on the same page. In thinking through how we approach the pending upgrade project, we determined that:*

- *There is a go versus no-go decision that's required before fully committing to the project.*

- *We determined there is risk of being unsupported and that the risk needs to be assessed in order to make the go versus no-go decision.*

- *Kristin's team will perform the risk assessment in time for our June 14th meeting so a go versus no-go decision can be made at that time.*

- *In the meantime, Jennifer's team will commence with planning activities so we don't fall too far behind if we make the decision to move forward.*

- *Did I miss anything?*

All: *We are good.*

Conversational summaries are commonly rich in meeting assets and are an essential part of the clarification process. You will notice from the example above that that the meeting manager's summary contained several meeting assets:

- Key Note—this upgrade is not a foregone conclusion and requires additional risk analysis before a final decision can be made.

- Risk—having unsupported software if the upgrade project takes too long.

- Action Item—Kristin and her team were tasked to perform the risk assessment by June 14th

- Decision—Jennifer will proceed with the upgrade project planning activities until a final decision is reached

Notice that a conversational summary is best approached from a bulleted or list perspective. This type of review simplifies communication and removes the temptation to add unnecessary verbiage. Remember our goal is alignment and clarity in the meeting communication so that everyone walks out of the meeting with a common understanding of who, what, where, when, why and how.

If you want to go further into mastering this meeting leader skill, we've got a great training

video for you at this link: http://meetingresult.com/psmmember.

This leads us to our final summarizing component—meeting summarizing.

Meeting Summarizing

Meeting summarizing is the ability to piece together the meeting assets and conversational summaries into a concise format that can be shared and referenced. Providing the concise notes without compromising the substance of a meeting is indeed a skill, which requires all the other skills we have discussed in order to put it into practice.

We covered the importance of meeting summarization and the meeting summary report in chapter four (meeting process). However it's important to reemphasize the fact that meeting summarizing is not synonymous with meeting minutes. While documenting minutes has a place in certain formal meeting structures, their value in most meeting contexts is questionable. Meeting minutes often have too much detail, take too long to prepare and are rarely even read.

Meeting summarizing is an essential component of PSM that functions to ensure clarity, alignment and accountability from meeting outcomes.

7 MEETING LEADER TRAITS

A genuine leader is not a searcher for consensus but a molder of consensus.

—Martin Luther King Jr.

If you examine the personality traits of great meeting leaders, certain key qualities stand out. The goal of this chapter is not to teach the reader how to exhibit these traits, but to raise awareness of the powerful characteristics inherent among these great leaders. While this list is by no means exhaustive, we hope it encourages you to perform an honest assessment of how you are showing up in three important areas. Regardless of where you stand, we believe these characteristics will help you develop a new approach for managing your meetings.

Humility

Humility is a characteristic that is often overlooked and arguably undervalued in corporate America. But when it comes to leading great business meetings, humility is an important personal asset. It refers to a leader who is not compelled to demonstrate that he is the smartest person in the room, even when he is.

Ironically, we see many cases where the smartest person in the room believes he possesses all the right answers and is ultimately a terrible listener.

In fact, humble leaders will allow themselves to ask the most basic questions to clarify an ambiguous comment and ensure attendees are being understood. The humble leader is comfortable letting everyone know that she doesn't understand the jargon or acronyms flying around the room, or even if she does, she will take time to clarify for the benefit of others who might not understand.

The humble meeting leader is self-deprecating enough to ask for the most fundamental explanations and knows that his understanding will also increase the probability of other attendees' understanding.

Humility is demonstrated in many different ways throughout the meeting process. It is an understanding that everyone in the room has an important role to play and deserves a voice (assuming you managed your attendance wisely). It is also a diligence in creating value for others by doing whatever is necessary to meet the objectives for the meeting while honoring and respecting stakeholders' time.

Confidence

Confidence is an obvious leadership trait in virtually any context. In a meeting leadership context, a confident leader creates an environment of assured attendees willing to follow the leader through the meeting process toward the objectives.

Think about it for a moment. How comfortable would you be climbing into a taxi with a seemingly nervous driver? Would you just sit back in your seat, or would you anxiously be looking over his shoulder with each passing turn? The same is true with meeting leaders. We need our attendees to know that we've got everything under control so they can focus on performing their role, not trying to drive the meeting.

A key component of the PSM system is the confidence that meeting leaders can enjoy by knowing they have a system that delivers continuously outstanding results.

Characteristics of a confident meeting leader include:

1. Optimizing Attendance

A confident meeting leader recognizes the importance of having the right people in the room to accomplish the meeting objectives. In many organizations it takes confidence to tell people they are not invited to a meeting that they would prefer to attend. It also takes confidence to tell higher-ranking executives that their attendance is *required*. A confident leader does what it takes to have the right people in attendance.

2. Keeping Attendees on Track

The meeting leader must be comfortable challenging and redirecting others in a professional manner to ensure they stay on track. He or she cannot be afraid (that is, lack the confidence) of ruffling feathers if attendees are heading off course, rambling, hijacking or otherwise deviating from the core meeting objectives.

3. Ensuring Clarity of Outcomes

Asking clarifying and or challenging questions to ensure clarity requires confidence. If an attendee is making a point that that is not clear, it becomes the meeting leader's responsibility to ask for clarification. This requires a level of candor and honesty that must be supported with confidence.

4. Enforcing Accountability

The meeting leader must be a shepherd of accountability and have the confidence to ensure that it is enforced. For example, every action item must have a corresponding owner. A meeting leader must have the confidence needed to ensure that action items are appropriately assigned and that due dates are established.

Organization

Meeting leaders set a tone for the meeting before a single attendee enters the meeting space. Basic actions, such as sending out a clear agenda with materials in advance of a meeting, demonstrate organization and competence. A meeting leader that plans on the fly, scrambles to prepare materials or has uncertainty about meeting participation sets a tone of disarray.

Organization involves simple tactics with high impact. Being an effective meeting manager requires a modest level of administrative work. Basic tasks, such as planning the agenda, making copies and confirming attendance, must always be done well. Failing to perform these tasks can undermine the effectiveness of the meeting.

Collectively humility, confidence and organization create a powerful formula for leaders leveraging the PSM system. These traits inspire attendees to perform at their best and enable the meeting leader to drive toward higher levels of clarity, accountability and performance that we so desperately need in our meeting rooms.

Remember to visit us at http://meetingresult.com/psmmember for exclusive training videos and resources for PSM readers.

8 GETTING STARTED

Do not let what you cannot do
interfere with what you can do.

—John Wooden

This book started with a deal. We agreed to share our best experiences and resources for conducting the most powerfully simple meetings. We hope you feel that we lived up to our end of the bargain, and we applaud you for dedicating your time and energy to consume the strategies and lessons contained herein. Now it's time for you to complete your end of the deal.

Now that you are equipped with a thorough understanding of the fundamental meeting challenges and the proven strategies for addressing them, where do you go from here? How do you continue the process of changing from your current state of meeting management, toward the future state of powerfully simple meetings (PSM)? Despite decades of failed attempts to fix unproductive meeting cultures, the answer is simpler than you would think.

As an equipped meeting leader, you now possess the tools for influencing the meeting practices in your organization. Individuals who decide to wait for an executive or corporate edict to mandate meeting productivity will likely wait a long time. The fact is that improving meeting culture is best accomplished from the ground up, one meeting at a time. In other words effective meeting management is best implemented as a "grass-roots" effort, and you now have the seeds to plant.

Your final step is to take the fundamentals you've learned in this book and apply them to your meetings from this day forward. Whether you are looking to implement PSM as an individual contributor, a small team, or across your enterprise, we recommend five key steps to help you implement PSM in your organization.

Step One—Evaluate Process Goals and Assets

The Business Process

Getting started begins with an evaluation of the core business process that you'll be supporting with your PSM system. Organizations leverage PSM to support business development processes, IT project management, executive leadership and governance, and the list goes on. PSM can be tailored to meet the specific needs of virtually any business process that relies on collaborative meetings to drive work forward.

Start by documenting the overarching goal of your business process (for example, your business development process, project management process), and the top three to five overall objectives of the meetings that support this process.

We've created a set of tools to assist you in your transition to the PSM system. All tools referenced throughout this chapter are available at: http://meetingresult.com/psmmember.

The following is sample output from this first step:

The overarching goals of our project management process is to ensure that our CRM system upgrade project is delivered by 12/31/14, within budget, with less than 24 hours of system downtime through conversion, and high stakeholder engagement throughout the change management process.

Key objectives of our project meeting process include:

- *Minimize the amount of time the development team members spend in meetings and away from their workstations*

- *Bridge the divide between IT and the Business by reinforcing alignment on scope, deliverables and accountability*

- *Drive rapid decision making that's needed to meet our aggressive delivery timeline*

- *Provide transparency on progress, action and decisions to key stakeholders to avoid any last-minute surprises (for example, misunderstood business requirements and expectations)*

With this information documented you're ready to evaluate and confirm the types of meeting assets you'll need to capture in these meetings.

The Assets

Once you've captured the overall goal and objectives for your business process meetings, you will want to confirm that you have the right asset model for your business process goals and meeting objectives.

As mentioned in chapter five, fundamental meeting assets for a standard meeting include action items, decisions, risks, issues, and key notes. This might be all the assets you're looking to capture from your meeting process (which seem appropriate for our example above), or you might want to define additional assets to support a unique process with distinctive meeting assets.

As a general rule, meetings typically surface between four and eight different asset types. Therefore, if you've identified more than a dozen different types of assets, you might be too granular in your approach and might consider grouping assets at a higher level. While it's certainly possible to have more than eight types of assets, that would be an exception rather than the general rule.

Refer to chapter five for a review about how to develop your own meeting asset types. Keep in mind that as you outline your assets, you will also need to identify what attributes you want to capture for each asset. For example, an action item would typically have a description, an owner and a due date.

To assist you we've created a complimentary tool to help you identify your meeting assets. Go to <u>http://meetingresult.com/psmmember</u> to access the asset identification tool.

You don't have to over-engineer this process, but it's important to be as clear as possible about what you're looking to capture during your meeting process.

Step Two—Stakeholder Analysis and Schedule

As you review the top three to five objectives for your meeting process and the asset types that you're looking to capture, your next step is to evaluate *who* needs to participate to contribute toward achieving the objectives of the meeting(s) and who needs to be informed of the meeting outcomes.

This step is about distinguishing between meeting attendees and meeting subscribers as discussed in chapter three. Remember that attendees are stakeholders who are essential to reaching your meeting objectives and executing your agenda. Subscribers are consumers of the content and need the information in order to be able to do their jobs.

We recognize that some meetings will require the list of attendees and subscribers to ebb and flow, but the goal here is to establish the baseline for your meeting process. Keep in mind that over participation in meetings is one of the five meeting killers and must be closely monitored to ensure we drive meeting performance and productivity.

The Schedule

The second part of this process is determining the meeting schedule needed to engage your stakeholders to achieve your overall meeting objectives. This includes defining your actual meeting schedule (for example, weekly, semi-monthly, ad hoc) and your expectations for delivering your meeting summary report to attendees and subscribers. The frequency of scheduling your meetings is fairly straightforward and will vary significantly based on your business process, organizational culture and schedule.

The timing of your meeting summary reporting warrants additional discussion. More advanced users of the PSM system might deliver a meeting summary report immediately following the completion of a meeting. Others might take more time to review and edit the summary report before distributing. As you focus on getting started with PSM, what's more important than the speed of delivery is the consistency of delivery. Keep in mind that your meeting subscribers are depending on this information to meet their needs, so providing them a predictable time that they will receive this information is essential. Otherwise we risk having them show up in the meetings again!

The general rule for distributing the meeting summary report is within forty-eight hours of your meeting (within twenty-four hours is ideal). However we recognize that this is not always possible. Quick reinforcement of meeting outcomes and accountability is critical so the sooner the better. As you proceed through this process, you'll see how rapidly your meeting subscribers (and attendees) will rely on the meeting summary reporting for their own uses.

Step Three—Tailor Your Process Tools

Before you begin leading your meetings using the PSM system you need to have your meeting process tools ready.

There are three essential tools that you need to have ready before conducting your first meeting:

1. Meeting Agenda

The agenda tool is the basic document that is used to communicate key information (for example, business objectives, agenda items, agenda item leaders, allocated time, attendees, subscribers and key logistical information) prior to the start of the meeting.

This tool establishes the meeting expectations and approach with attendees. While this is a simple tool, don't underestimate the importance of leveraging each of the components contained in it.

As you get started with PSM, it's essential that you distribute the agenda well in advance of the meeting (ideally at least twenty-four hours ahead of time) to allow attendees the opportunity to review and prepare.

Visit http://meetingresult.com/psmmember to download a complimentary meeting agenda template for your use.

2. Meeting Execution Dashboard

The execution dashboard tool is at the heart of your meeting execution process. It includes the space to quickly capture your identified meeting assets and related attributes, meeting attendance and other progress made during the course of your meeting. This document becomes the basis for your meeting summary report that will be communicated to all stakeholders.

As a reminder, PSM readers get an exclusive offer to try our Web-based meeting management software. The software provides a Meeting Execution Dashboard for you to leverage. Just go to http://meetingresult.com/psmmember to learn more.

3. Meeting Summary Report

The meeting summary report is the essential output delivered from each of your business meetings. It builds from your agenda and meeting execution dashboard to provide the "document of record" for your meeting.

Visit http://meetingresult.com/psmmember to download a complimentary meeting summary report template for your use.

This document is the essential tool you'll leverage to reinforce accountability and clarification of meeting outcomes, inform meeting subscribers of important meeting information, and provide the historical record to assist you in the weeks and months ahead.

Step Four—Equip Your Stakeholders

Before you begin running your meetings, it's also important to equip your stakeholders with the basic information they need to engage in your PSM system. After all, your meetings are changing so it's in your best interest to inform them upfront.

Templates for the tools outlined below are available at <u>http://meetingresult.com/psmmember</u>.

There are three available tools to help you engage your stakeholders before conducting your first meeting:

1. Stakeholder Communication

The stakeholder communication tool is a simple communication that you can send to the individuals involved in your meeting process. It provides an overview of the PSM system and establishes expectations for what stakeholders will experience while utilizing this new meeting process (for example, how meetings will be conducted, communication of meeting output). This communication should also reference a job aid for stakeholders to learn more about the system.

2. Stakeholder Job Aid

We recommend providing a simple job aid for stakeholders to reference during the meeting process. This document builds from the initial stakeholder communication but provides a more in depth overview of the PSM system. Leverage this tool to ensure your stakeholders have all the information that they need to interact successfully with your new meeting process.

3. Stakeholder Presentation

The final step for equipping stakeholders is to allocate time during your first couple of meetings to cover the highlights of the new meeting process. The goal here is to reinforce the changes that you're making, why you're making them and expectations of the stakeholders as they interact with the process. We provide a presentation template for you to tailor and leverage during your initial meetings.

Step Five—Launch and Adjust

At last you are ready to complete the final step toward getting started, launching and adjusting your PSM system. It's important to keep in mind that your process will likely need to be refined over the course of time (hence the adjust). Rarely do our clients get this system perfect on the first try. So going into this step with a "launch-and-adjust" mindset is helpful. It's also helpful to set those expectations with your meeting stakeholders and allow them the opportunity to contribute to any needed adjustments.

After you've executed a critical mass of meetings (that is, a minimum of three to five), you're ready to assess your process and make any needed adjustments. Ask yourself the following questions:

- Do we have the right stakeholders (attendees and subscribers) identified?

- Are we capturing the right asset types?

- Are we effectively capturing assets for inclusion in the meeting summary report?

- Do stakeholders understand the meeting process?

- Are stakeholders buying into the process? (this can take a while, so give it time)

- Is the meeting summary report effectively utilized?

- What other adjustments would make this process better?

The answers to these questions will lead you back to steps one and two of the getting-started process. Simply make the necessary adjustments and incorporate them into the meeting process. Then you will develop a tailored meeting system that will allow you to execute the most productive meetings imaginable.

9 MEETING TECHNOLOGY

It is only through enforced standardization of methods,
enforced adoption of the best implements and
working conditions, and enforced cooperation that
faster work can be assured.

—Frederick Winslow Taylor

Frederick Winslow Taylor is regarded as the father of scientific management and a pioneer of management consulting. His ideas can be found in many performance management theories and systems in existence today and his concept of the "One Best Way" to do work can be applied in virtually any industry or business context.

"One Best Way" grew out of Taylor's belief that the "system" was the most important aspect of any business. This belief foreshadowed a time when people would simply follow well-defined business systems in order to generate predictable results. The assembly line, the layout of kitchens, the way libraries function and the operation of fast-food restaurants all owe much to Frederick Taylor and his concept of the "One Best Way." He truly believed that if you studied work you could develop a process that would capture the best way to perform that work to maximize efficiency and results. If Taylor was alive today there is no doubt he would agree that meetings are excellent candidates for the application of his "One Best Way" concept.

Our meetings are ripe for standardization of methods and practices for making them more efficient and effective. Throughout this book we have raised awareness of the root cause problems (that is, meeting killers) that plague business meetings. We laid out our PSM system for neutralizing these meeting killers and restoring meetings as a valuable communications tool for moving your business forward. The key components of PSM we covered include:

- Guiding Principles—the foundation on which all PSM is based.

- Meeting Process—the steps and strategies (for example, meeting assets) for executing consistently outstanding business meetings.

- Leader Skills and Traits—the core competencies and skills possessed by the best meeting leaders.

- Plan for Getting Started—the strategy and steps for beginning the PSM process in your organization.

PSM can be implemented as a manual process and you will experience a transformation of your meetings into highly effective vehicles that help you advance your business and engage your teams. In fact the authors of this book leveraged PSM as a manual process for years! However, as with many other business system innovations (such as accounting, inventory management or human resources), information technology holds the key to unlocking exponentially greater efficiencies that are otherwise unattainable using manual processes.

Computers and software have revolutionized the way organizations conduct business and continue to have a profound effect on the productivity of workers and organizations. Airlines and banking are two businesses where information technology has proven absolutely essential. Without technology handling the vast amount of information and analysis, the functions these industries perform would be nearly impossible. Imagine if a bank tried to keep track of all its customer financial data without the use of computer systems to help manage the information and ensure that it is available to service customers in a timely manner.

Businesses of all types have used technology to automate their processes and provide the ability to scale operations while keeping control of critical elements of the business through the use of information technology. More recently the concept of "Big Data" has come to the forefront and organizations are starting to harness massive stores of information to gain key insights into business performance, customer preferences and to manage risk and perform complex "what-if" analysis.

Once we developed PSM, we wanted to know how we could make it better, faster and simpler using information technology. That led us to designing and developing a technology platform to automate and streamline as much of the meeting process as feasible. Our goal was to zero in on the "One Best Way" to conduct the most powerfully simple business meetings possible.

We started small with a simple mobile application and we spent more than two years crowdsourcing requirements and obtaining feedback from thousands of users. We expanded our offering and today we offer our technology solution in the Cloud, on mobile devices and as a turnkey appliance that you can deploy in your own data center and be up and running immediately. By wrapping PSM in technology, we significantly amplify and accelerate the results that meeting leaders and organizations can achieve.

As a PSM reader, we invite you to leverage our Web-based application. We have an exclusive offer for our readers, so just go to

http://meetingresult.com/psmmember for more information.

With all the advances in information technology, it is mind-boggling that so little has been done to bring technology into the meeting space. By using our MeetingResult technology platform to automate our PSM System there are four key benefits that you will realize:

1. Efficient Meeting Data Capture

MeetingResult technology provides a means for efficient meeting planning, critical meeting information capture and distribution and archival of meeting agenda information, meeting assets and meeting summary reports.

- Plan your agenda with a standardized input form or clone a previous meeting and make changes. Planning data includes meeting logistics (date/time, location), objective(s), agenda items, speaking notes, attendees and meeting subscribers.

- Create a professionally formatted agenda and calendar invite with a single click.

- Track attendance against list of attendees with a single click.

- Capture meeting assets (key notes, action items, decisions, issues and risks) identified during the meeting using standardized input forms.

- Create a meeting summary report with a single click.

2. Streamline Meeting Follow-Up Activities

Once a meeting is completed, the work to manage the follow-up activities and extract the maximum value begins. The follow-through on the meeting is essential to ensure that the time invested in the meeting is leveraged as much as possible. The MeetingResult technology platform makes it easy to handle follow-up activities by automating much of the tasks.

- Email reminders are automatically sent to owners of action items, issues, and risks at the conclusion of a meeting.

- Information is automatically sent via email to anyone tagged on a meeting asset during a meeting.

- Single-click access to update status on meeting assets via web-based forms.

- Real-time status updates automatically available to meeting leaders.

3. Automated Reporting / Analytics

Once meeting data has been captured in the system it can automatically be used to drive reporting and analytics. The ability to quickly run reports for single meetings and all meetings for a given project or initiative allows you to keep tabs on project performance through the lens of meetings. The analytics and reporting included in the MeetingResult technology platform allows you to answer important questions like:

- What is the average attendance percentage for my meetings?

- How many person hours have we invested in meetings this year?

- Are my meetings decision oriented (number of decisions made), action oriented (number of action items assigned) or strictly informational (number of key notes captured)?

- How many action items assigned during meetings were completed on time?

- How many action items assigned during meetings are overdue?

- Who owns action items that are overdue? Is there one person or several people who are not completing items most frequently?

While these are some of obvious questions of interest to a project manager, there are many ways to analyze the data to gain insights into meeting performance.

The important takeaway is that the MeetingResult technology platform captures and utilizes your meeting data in a single repository so that you can answer important questions about your meeting performance.

4. Collaboration Hub

Meetings involve collaboration and communication before, during and after the actual time spent in the meeting room. The best meetings foster a sense of collaboration and communication that lets ideas flourish and provide clear communication around important topics related to your projects and business.

The MeetingResult technology platform functions as a central hub for communications surrounding your meetings. It begins the minute you decide to have the meeting and ends once all post-meeting, follow-up activities have been completed. The system provides a means to share information among the meeting leader and the attendees. Updates to information occur in real time and are accessible from mobile and Cloud-based interfaces.

The MeetingResult technology platform allows people external to the meeting to be looped into the conversation by providing them with information automatically either by tagging them on certain items or including them as a subscriber to a meeting.

These are just some of the immediate benefits that you will realize by using the MeetingResult technology platform to automate our PSM system. Throughout the long term we know that you will come to rely on the MeetingResult technology platform as an essential tool in your daily workflow. The meeting knowledge base that you will build with each meeting conducted will provide you with the ability to search through your meetings and quickly locate important information, such as important decisions made and who was in attendance at key meetings. These and many other details are quickly forgotten or lost using manual processes for managing meetings.

We have only scratched the surface of the benefits that can be obtained from applying information technology to the process of managing meetings. The most important thing that you can do now is to ask yourself an important question.

How do you currently manage your meetings?

Are you still using a pen and notebook to keep track of important meeting information? Maybe you have moved to taking notes in a Word document or some other word-processing program. There is nothing wrong with either of these methods but neither of them is the "One Best Way" to manage meetings.

Anyone tasked with handling accounting for a business, even a small business, would hardly choose a spreadsheet to keep track of all of the company's financial data and manually create profit-and-loss statements. There are lots of accounting technology platforms on the market that can automatically pull bank and credit-card transactions, create and email invoices, track receivables and expenses and create profit and loss and other reports with a single click. The time savings realized from using one of the accounting systems more than pays for the cost of the system.

How much is your time worth? Are you wasting precious time trying to manually keep track of important meeting information? How much more productive and organized would you be if you had a system to automate and keep track of your meeting information? The MeetingResult technology platform provides you with the same type of efficiency gains that are realized with accounting systems.

Your time is too valuable. Stop managing meetings with pen and paper and other manually intensive processes. We have spent thousands of hours developing PSM and automating it with the MeetingResult technology platform. You can take advantage of all this work and start having fewer, faster, more focused meetings today.

Visit http://meetingresult.com/psmmember to learn more.

If you would like to learn more about our enterprise training and technology solutions, please send us an email at info@meetingresult.com.

ABOUT THE AUTHORS

BRYAN FIELD is a senior information technology executive and cofounder of MeetingResult LLC. He has more than sixteen years of experience in Software and Systems Development, IT Security, Business Process Reengineering and Web and Mobile Technology Implementations and has worked extensively in both the federal government and private sector. Before cofounding MeetingResult, Mr. Field built and led a sales organization for a defense contractor. He received his bachelor of science degree in Industrial and Systems Engineering from Virginia Tech and has been a certified project management professional (PMP) since 2005.

PETER KIDD is a strategic project manager and corporate executive with twenty years of comprehensive knowledge within the Project Management, Human Resources, Finance and Accounting and Enterprise Resource Planning fields. Mr. Kidd has extensive experience managing enterprise transformation initiatives, most recently at Sodexo Inc. and Freddie Mac. He received his bachelor of science degree in Accounting from The Pennsylvania State University and is a certified project management professional (PMP). Mr. Kidd is also a formally trained executive coach, having received his professional training from Columbia University in New York.

BRYAN, left; PETER, right

41884529R00084

Made in the USA
Middletown, DE
25 March 2017